Dimitris N. Chorafas

PETROCELLI BOOKS

Princeton, New Jersey

Library of Congress Cataloging-in-Publication Data

Chorafas, Dimitris N.
    Interactive workstations.

    Bibliography: p.
    Includes index.
    1. Microcomputers. 2. Interactive computer systems.
I. Title.
QA76.5.C4797 1986   658.4'038   86–5123
ISBN 0-89433-258-9

CONTENTS

INTRODUCTION

A book is written for a certain purpose. The purpose of this text is to explain the current state-of-the-art in designing and implementing workstations. When it comes to computers and communications, business and industry finds itself at a crossroad. Personal computing is one of the key reasons. Decisions made today will commit a company for the next 10 years. The *how* and *why* is properly explained through this book.

It is a sad fact with modern industrial life that the higher up one climbs in an organization, the less sophisticated is the information equipment at his disposal. As a concept and as a realization, workstations for the executive aim to correct this imbalance. They are small but powerful, dedicated systems that are easy to use. By relieving users of routine work, workstations improve personal productivity. This in turn increases the benefits an organization can derive from their implementation.

The management of a company must transform the potential benefit of technology into reality while taking into account the corporate objectives, managerial styles, industrial trends, level of competition and state of the economy. Communications specialists must provide the technical solutions to reach the goals management puts across.

This book is written in an easy-to-follow manner and presupposes no background in computers. Both senior managers and computer specialists can gain from these chapters.

This book is based on facts. If at times it goes beyond "proven" notions it is because people project linearly, but growth phenomena are expotential. We have to account for this fact.

Let me close by expressing my thanks to everybody who contributed to this book: to my colleagues for their insight and to Eva-Maria Binder for the drawings, typing and index.

Dimitris N. Chorafas
Valmer and Vitznau

Chapter **1**

EFFECTIVELY USING THE WORKSTATION

Introduction

The computer system is an increasingly vital element of a company's differentiation. By 1986, advances in artificial intelligence, expert systems, interactive videodiscs, laser technology and most particularly *personal computers* are changing the landscape of old data processing.

Users have become knowledgeable. *They want solutions* and they also require that their computer systems pay for themselves with greater personal productivity and efficiency. *This means multifunctional, communicating workstations.* Said Victor Millar, managing partner of Arthur Anderson*: "Well over half of our business this year (1985) involved executive-level computing, which is up significantly from five years ago." And on December 10, 1985, a Paine Webber Status Report suggested: "With the help of personal computers we have changed our method of tracking quarterly results for the 21 companies we follow most closely."

Personal computing is used for wide range of activities: calculating, electronic mail, word processing (WP), document storage, search and retrieval of information, communications with databases. It is used as an analytical tool, for exception reporting, for graphical presentation, and for more traditional activities such as accounting, planning, and scheduling. It provides the executive with calendar services and online monitoring capabilities for control purposes. It offers the systems specialist a powerful tool for program development, and is for both the manager and specialist an important learning aid.

Personal computing is done at the *workstation* (WS)—the intelligent, programmable workstation (as we will treat it in this chapter).

---

*The Christian Science Monitor, December 6, 1985.

■ 1

Workstations are often confused with *terminals*. This is a poor policy as terminals can be:

dumb,

smart, or

intelligent.

The latter can serve as workstations and are usually powered by personal computers (PC). Intelligent terminals have different degrees of functioning ability:

dumb connections in emulation of dumb terminals

local storage for downloading, with only error control

structure and formatting of downloaded data

local work on data where the term *personal computing* can be applied

local formatting prior to upline sending

microfile handling on a file access basis

microfiles with DBMS capability

use of DBMS as a programming language at run time

variety of communications protocols

Simultaneous processing and communications with one or more mainframes.

The critical questions is: "What can the WS do for executives and professionals?" What are we to do with more microprocessor power embedded into the executive desk? To answer this we must take a systems view, and we must also look into the main trends in WS design.

Implementing the Workstation

The personal computing revolution, like other revolutions before it, will be assimilated into front office and back office operations. Unlike other events, it will also reach the executive desk and boardroom.

By December 31, 1985, an estimated 90% of the country's largest companies are involved in end user computing. By 1990, nearly half

Table 1.1 Projections on usage of installed PC at WS level.	
UPPER MANAGEMENT	15%
MIDDLE MANAGEMENT	41%
OTHER PROFESSIONALS	14%
SECRETARIAL/CLERICAL	30%
	100%

of all the computer power in the U.S. will be devoted to end user computing—which will be reaching the 75% level of installed power before the end of the century.

An end user computing system exists when the end user has ownership of the application. By early 1986 less than 5% of major applications on mainframes have been end user oriented. True end user computing is made through WS and has more to do with the type of products that exist on *information center* environments.

This is a major change. Therefore, projections and statistics can be valuable. Table 1.1 presents projections on end usage. The U.S. Automobile Association in San Antonio, Texas, expects that all of its 5,500 employees will soon be using WS.

Though this may not be the typical case, the trend suggests that by 1989 *at least 65% of all professionals* will have more than one PC and the 32 BPW will dominate. A 32 BPW micro has a capability at the level of an IBM 4341—a lot of power for personal computing.

By increasing the power of the microcomputer family, suppliers further the role of the PC in a commercial environment. By the end of this decade, WS will be designed around the new generation of microcomputers. Professionals will be asking for 32-BPW machines, megabytes of central memory, interactive graphics, and sophisticated decision support models. Here is what the WS should be doing for the executive and the professional in the coming years:

1. Multimedia support.

Traditionally, the computer service offered to the executive has been based on data. Now, we must integrate text and graphics. For graphics, we think originally of output but we also look increasingly at input. Image processing capability and speech input/output will also be important.

2. Communications—both local and long haul.

The importance of engines able to communicate among themselves and with databases is becoming more evident every day. Decision support systems rest 90% on data and only 10% on mathematics.

Text and data are distributed. Computing is only a small part of the total. Within this environment there are plenty of opportunities for communications, with a trend developing toward embedding the communications capability into the micro hardware itself.

3. Database distribution, from microfiles (personal files) to central text and data warehouses.

In this decade, both processing and databases will be distributed to the lowest levels of the organization—subject to two factors: The need to integrate data at levels above the lowest; and the necessity of operating at WS and local area network (LAN) levels without professional operators.

Among the system prerequisites are the need to reorganize the supporting databases, to review the data acquisition and reporting system, to accommodate management interactivity requirements, and to reassign organizational responsibilities in the process. The same is true of realigning functional responsibilities affecting both line and staff at all levels.

As any reorganization will necessarily proceed in stages, the system study should provide the capability for producing both old and new information to bridge the transition. This will improve the level of understanding of the new systems, reduce resistance, and increase the capability of comparative evaluations.

With these prerequisites satisfied, by 1990 about three-quarters of the installed computer power in an organization will be integrated into executive, professional and clerical desks as Figure 1.1 document.

4. Flexibility for expanding future requirements.

Requirements for more power, greater central memory, and hard disc support are growing every day. Resolution at the level of the video display has become a key issue in handling data, text, and graphics.

5. Software ergonomics

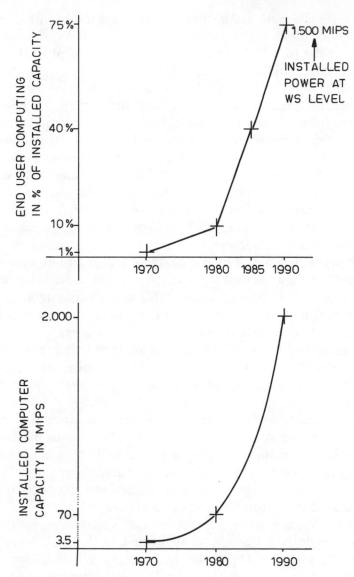

Figure 1.1 Statistics and forecasts by a leading firm for its own operations.

Many issues come under this heading: the facility of use; the ability to learn the system easily; the support of help functions; adaptability; consistency in design; and security.

The system should ensure that a small mistake by the user does not become a disaster. This capability is software-based and consumes machine cycles (of which the intelligent terminal has plenty).

Ergonomic considerations are important as, till now, the user has had to sit at the computer keyboard and type-in arcane and hard-to-remember commands to make his machine work. Every time he wanted to change from one job to another, he had to change program discs. To make things worse, the information he typed into one program had to be typed in again if he needed to use it in another program.

With the WS, the user interacts through easy media—touch screens, tablets, joysticks, a mouse, and eventually a voice—to feed in text/data and get responses. Furthermore, as we will see in further chapters, fourth generation programming languages tremendously ease the job of commanding the computer.

Anybody who has ever used a personal computer knows that user interfaces leave a great deal of room for improvement. The result has been the *mouse/window* concept—also known as the desktop metaphor—in which the computer screen is segmented into a number of windows containing various pieces of work in progress.

In a good implementation, data can be transferred from window to window with a few flicks of a mechanical pointing device, such as a mouse! The way the mouse/window works is transparent to the end-user.

The manufacturer, however, knows that developing a mouse/window operating system is the easy part. Developing elegant data interchange capabilities and good application development tools for window systems is the real challenge. Once done, they can be used to produce further new applications or modify existing ones. We have finally moved away from throw-away software.

Modern, programmable workstations are visual display units containing a single board computer dedicated to the application being executed by the user. This is the most concise WS definition, and it conforms to what we have said so far. Figure 1.2 brings under perspective the range of peripherals a WS can have.

Applications programs should be retained on the microfile (on hard disc) and loaded over the bus to the central memory when called by the user. They should then execute under a single user executive in the workstation.

Workstations should communicate among themselves through a LAN—and long haul. Every new user allocated a slot in the communi-

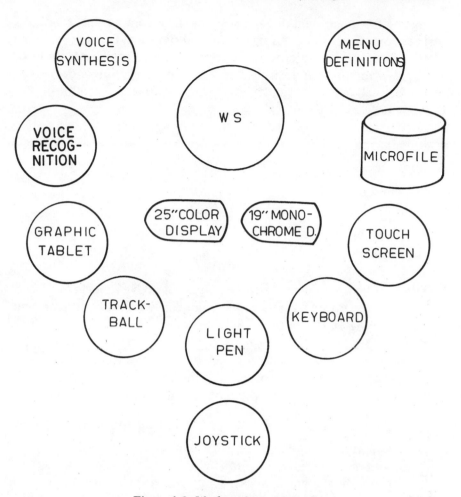

Figure 1.2 Workstation peripherals.

cations domain adds a processor to the overall system, thus increasing the total processing power, rather than causing further dilution of a central processor resource assigned to running applications code (as with mainframes and minis).

Advantages with WS Implementation

A key advantage of the PC is that it supplies lots of central processing unit (CPU) cycles for the user. Minis and mainframes have a hard time doing so for many simultaneous users, and communications links further complicate the job if operated without local PC support.

Without powerful microcomputers with local intelligence able to access information, the justification for online computers decreases. PCs effectively reduce the entry-level price to the mainframe world.

WS software lets the user do:

graphing,

word processing,

calculating,

drawing,

list creation, and

project scheduling.

Results can be brought to the top of a pile of active reports or placed underneath for future reference. Data can easily be exchanged among all jobs running on the WS.

The user can tell his workstation what to do, for instance, by pointing to one of the commands listed across the top of the screen. The pointer arrow can be moved by a mouse, or joystick. A click of the button activates the chosen command and a set of follow-up instructions appears.

Housekeeping chores are represented by small pictures on the screen—data, for example, can be thrown away when clicked into the *wastebasket* or saved on a *clipboard*.

In a properly designed workplace, the workstations should be installed in existing desks; more precisely, mounted under the desks with the keyboard, numeric keypad or graphic tablet, as well as the video display installed on the desktops.

This arrangement is advantageous because desktops are normally used for other clerical functions and space is at a premium. Furthermore, WS design is practically synonymous to that of the workplace and the possibility of steady enhancements should be one of the critical factors.

For example, a system originally designed for alphanumerical presentation may have to be converted to graphics through the incorporation of a module supporting the generation of rasterscan alphageometric output, providing a wide range of bandwidth, resolution, and visual dynamics under program control. Steady computer support is crucial for user-oriented features:

help and prompt features

color, graphics

displaying multiple windows

WP and electronic mail

spreadsheet processing

microfile management

database programming.

Supported features must be totally transparent to the end-user who only cares for the final output—but they should be of concern to the system specialist. He should be interested in incorporating devices with programmable delay and registers, allowing the data chosen by the user to be displayed at any point in the video frame.

The specialist should ensure that the output of several video formatters can be superimposed to form more complex pictures. The user should only know how to employ such facilities, calling into play the commands he needs to do this job.

The design of the workplace should incorporate user-friendly devices both for input and for presentation. With appropriate programming, local processing becomes an easy-to-fulfill requirement. Each micro runs its own copy of basic and applications software and acts as an independent WS.

A change occurs when a user wants to access an information element residing in the file server. The file server does the bidding of the WS, providing it with the requested data record, file, or program. To the WS there is no difference between retrieving data from a local storage device (microfile) or from the file server.

This approach has several advantages over the typical centralized multiuser system. When several dumb terminals share a single processor, users are served only as long as the processor can cope with the demands of all users within a short response time. However, as more users are added, the processor gets overloaded and each suffers a slowdown in terminal response.

To the contrary, with a LAN each WS has its own processor and operating system, so there is no slowdown in computation as additional units are added to the network. The file server handles all software needed to control access to the local area database. It offers networks a higher level of sophistication by responding to WS requests on a file basis.

Another reason for sharing a resource is the need to make common information accessible from multiple workstations. Thus, a file server shares a relatively large, expensive disc-based memory and makes available the information stored on this database.

Small micro files might be maintained on a workstation hard disc, but large or generally accessible files are owned by the file server. The latter must coordinate concurrent access to a given file. A sophisticated facility supports such additional services as file sorting, catalog management, archiving, and index searching.

Another aspect in information science is that of the coming *logical desks*. By 1990, the electronic desks typically represented by today's WS will change into logical desks. Pocket-size PCs with microfiles and communications protocols will permit work on business trips, interactivity at meetings and seminars, beginning the workday at home, no distractions on evenings and weekends, and work on projects with people in other locations and time zones.

A Multifunctional Workstation

The idea of a multifunctional WS develops on two premises. First, an increasing number of users demand integrated WS—not single-job-oriented machines. Second, these machines have become microprocessor based—and therefore intelligent—with lots of internal memory at the WS level.

Multifunctional WS require significant local abilities, hence the use of personal computers rather than stupid terminals. This implies more software support, a greater sophistication in OS, and native communications capabilities.

The WS will typically be a PC with spreadsheet or integrated software. The user—usually no professional programmer—can nicely work with a fourth generation programming language to answer his own needs, while he may find difficulty in manipulating the finer programmatic interfaces of classical programming solutions.

However, sprawling, independent PCs can turn company communications into a jungle. Systems integration perspectives are therefore needed to assure that all component parts will be properly coordinated aggregate.

At any and every WS, the PC is part of a larger integrated system. In this capacity it can act as both a personal computing facility and terminal of the larger interconnected aggregate. But the user is the same. He doesn't care where the text, data, and graphics come from or where the program is executing. To make the user interface *consistent* is a difficult job and needs lots of work to be accomplished.

Developing the proper interfaces calls for significant software and datacomm expertise. One basic issue is to provide forms that are consistent and can be handled in the same format at all levels of processing/ databasing: PC, mini, mainframes. This is particularly valid when we talk of corporate files (softcopy and hardcopy, input and output). Within a distributed information system, the format must be pre-designed and fully distributed. The forms must be as universally applicable as possible.

Another issue to be given proper thought is *encryption*. This is nothing more than a software means to increase hardware security due to distributed resources. We must ensure that nobody will break into files and that protected data is never shared by any other unauthorized point in the network.

Challenges with PC Implementation

The effects of growth in corporate personal computer use are overwhelmingly perceived to be positive—increasing productivity and providing users with faster access to results. However, in the short term, major problems may occur. Some are a natural result of a sudden increase in the perceived benefits of the systems.

The first risk is an explosion in purchasing without providing the framework for their selection, acquisition, and integration. The second risk is the use of old concepts in handling the new engines. This may range from applications development and the use of languages to the handling of the network.

Programming is an area of particular sensitivity. A brief reference has been made to *fourth generation programming languages* (4GL), also known as *very high level languages* (VHLL). These can be classified in five major groups, top to bottom:

1. Programming extensions to the OS through a command interpreter
2. Database management and query
3. New programming languages (artificial intelligence and graphics)
4. Productivity oriented tools (through precompilers)
5. Spreadsheet systems.

Spreadsheet systems are particularly appealing to the end-user, provided the end user is able to define his role and knows how to use the tool. This is not self-evident.

Training programs for managers and professionals, with hands-on experience, are being instituted by many organizations to help in this direction. A good example is the training program developed in 1985 by Honeywell Information Technology Center (ITC) and MicroTraining Associates of Boston.

The program is designed so that participants would acquire two qualities:

1. The confidence to apply the new skills (PC, spreadsheets, online to database), and
2. A reference tool that serves as a reminder of how to accomplish specific tasks.

The objective of the course is to help participants understand, learn and do. Quite importantly, during the course *participants spend 90% of their time learning by doing on the interactive workstation*. That's how to teach people about PC, spreadsheets, electronic mail, and online access to databases.

Results are self-evident if we consider the fact that 78% of the participants stated that the hands-on training had a positive or outstanding impact on their ability to use the machine. Only under this condition can we say that spreadsheets are a great idea, and their scope is one that goes far beyond doing financial operations. In fact, they are an excellent way to program the machine if the user masters this skill.

Personalized results can be obtained through the use of spread-sheet capabilities and of database programming languages. Individual applications, unsurprisingly, are state-of-the-art.

The mouse and window permit menus and help screens of un-matched functionality. Most impressive of all is the level of product integration. As one example, spreadsheets can be linked to an essentially unlimited degree while still maintaining their individual simplicity and integrity.

Another issue within the broader implementation perspective, is the redistribution of tasks. Editing tasks now performed on the main-frame can be offloaded. PCs should serve as local transaction editors. The same is valid of interactive reporting procedures.

DP management must become conscious of the advantages of personal systems for ad hoc applications. They are easy to use where there are reasonable amounts of data involved. So, the results come quicker and in a more comprehensive form.

The favorable attitude toward PCs is mirrored by a general expectation that their use will ease the burdens of DP management in the long term. However, the job may be made more difficult in the short term, primarily because of user unfamiliarity with programs and data controls.

Yet, even without PCs, the growing wave of online solutions and end-user computing will overwhelm the DP department unless the latter is prepared for it. By the end of the decade, PC power integrated in WS will represent *three times* the number of CPU cycles imbedded in classical data processing.

The broad range of communications necessary to sustain our society is shown in Figure 1.3, and is expanded upon below.

Electronic Funds Transfer (EFT)
1. Automated teller machines (ATM)
2. Point of sales (POS) equipment
3. Check-credit verification
4. Electronic cash registers
5. Long haul funds transfer

Home Banking (HB)
6. Account information
7. Client orders

Merchandising

    8. Video catalogues

    9. Teleshopping

Travel

   10. Schedules

   11. Reservations

Entertainment

   12. Teleguides

   13. Bookings

Other Information Providers (IP)

   14. One-way advertising

   15. Weather reports

   16. Stock market prices

   17. Real-time news

   18. Telephone directories

   19. Lessons

   20. Specialized databases

Office and Home Links

   21. PC-to-host switching

   22. Communicating databases

   23. Classical voice networks

   24. Video phones

   25. Facsimile

   26. Image handling

   27. Local area networks (LAN)

   28. Metropolitan area networks (MAN)

   29. Value added networks (VAN)

   30. Electronic Mail

   31. Telex/TWX

   32. Other message switching systems

Typically, the WS will be the polyvalent terminal device to such networks able to handle both transactions and interactive queries.

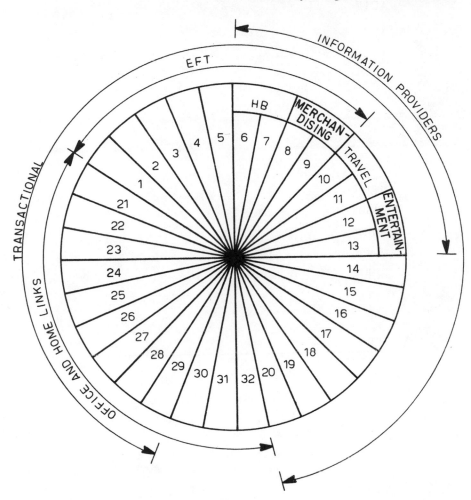

Figure 1.3 Information universe for online communications.

Computers and communications will make a large contribution to problem-solving, but the success or failure of the operation will primarily rest with the person behind the machine.

Chapter 2

THE BEGINNING OF 32-BIT WORKSTATIONS

Introduction

The first 32-BPW personal computer to be offered at less than $3,000 is Apple's Macintosh, an early 1984 announcement. It signals the beginning of a third generation of workstations. The first PC generation was characterized by 8-BPW engines, a typical case being Apple II. The second used 16-BPW engines, with the IBM PC being the market winner.

Altogether, a significant evolution has taken place along the twelve mainlines of reference identified in Table 2.1.

There are many things a 16-BPW engine can do faster than an 8-BPW. An important reference is the memory addressing capability. The 16 BPW has a largely expanded range beyond the 64 KB that has been standard with 8 BPW. This means:

more complex programs

larger working storage

higher processing speeds

less disc accessing.

A similar statement can be made in contrasting 16-BPW and 32-BPW engines, with graphics attracting most interest.

The market is voting with dollars. Computer buyers care about technical achievement, continuity, compatibility, and customer support. Significant technical achievements can attract consumers away from the most deeply entrenched standards.

In the late 1960s, the minicomputer emerged and captured a sizable portion of the mainframe market.

In the late 1970s, the 8-BPW PC took business away both from dumb mainframe-based terminals and from minis.

Table 2.1 Three generations of PCs and Supermicros.
Between 1979 and 1986, 12 key factors have changed:
1. *Microprocessors* (8, 16, 32 BPW)
2. *Central memory* (64K, 256K, 1 MB, 4 MB)
3. *Auxiliary memory* (Floppy 8″, 5 1/2″, 3 1/2″; HD 0, 30 MB, 60 MB)
4. *Video display* (0.2, 0.5; 1 mega Pixel)
5. *OS* (CPM, MS DOS, Unix, VM)
6. *DBMS* (KRAM (FM), DBase II, Ingres, Oracle)
7. *Integrated software* (successively more sophisticated generations)
8. *Programming languages* (Cobol, Pascal, "C," DBase II, III, others)
9. *End-user functionality* (keyboard, menus, help, prompts, mouse, graphic tablet, popup menus, voice I/O)
10. *Graphics support* (2-D, 3-D, color, icons, document handling, moving pictures)
11. *Communications capabilities* (classical packages; PCB, new protocols, multicommunications aggregate)
12. *LAN connectivity* (BAB, BRB, born BIU).

In 1981, the 16-BPW PC cut into the 8-BPW market and eventually killed the 8-bit micro.

In 1984, this has been repeated with the 32-BPW engines—whether as supermicro at the expense of the mini or as intelligent WS for personal computing.

In 1986 we experience both a plurality of offers featuring 32-BPW and a minor price now which makes this formerly expensive engine widely affordable.

The latter thrust takes advantage of the increased power of the latest generation of silicon chips, new software, and fourth generation programming languages. This pace will accelerate by capitalizing on the next generation of very high capacity semiconductors.

Functional Integration

Operating systems (OS) for personal computers have greatly evolved in terms of concept and functionality. One reference is from monotasking to multitasking. Another rests on the fact that even CPM 80 and MS DOS presents features not included in some of the OS currently available for mainframes.

The new generation of personal workstations honors the Turing philosophy of keeping hardware simple. The foundation of this new line is to solve one's problem by means of much thought—rather than by throwing money and equipment at the problem.

This is precisely what the new generation of integrated software aims to do. The facilities which it supports provide an ordered solution to a set of thorny technical problems.

Most PC users tend to use one type of program at a time. The challenge lies in the ability to switch from one program to the next in a way transparent to the end-user. At the same time, PC customers expect more than they are getting. This brings up the notion of a total professional computing environment with a significant simplification of procedures for changing applications programs.

Most end-users do not want to program, and they should not get involved in programming. They will, however, use packages or application generators for PCs. Integrated approaches—from the management of the computer resources to the applications program itself—provide the solutions:

Multiple user views of text, data, and graphics,

simplified user interfaces,

faster implementation of applications and relative changes of the user's choice

are the issues which have the greatest potential for market appeal. Such issues have *not* been solved with mainframes, nor with minis. Therefore, they are challenging subjects with PCs.

Another critical PC reference is to be connected to central hosts in a network. This involves not only data link protocols but also (in a professional environment) synchronization of updates, bulk data transfers and database failure detection and recoverability. The casual PC user may not care about that (though he will be concerned about his ability to communicate with public databases) but the professional PC user has such facilities now—and the OS in its most extended view must provide them.

Synchronous binary file transfers are possible through 3270 emulation products, but they are not enough. The integrated PC-to-host link must solve data flow problems by automatically converting mainframe data into information the microcomputer packages can use—and vice versa.

This greatly involves the new OS concept in an integrated software sense. Though the micro to mainframe link may, for instance, support one spreadsheet, it must be possible to get the transferred data into other spreadsheets through an intermediate file in a standard format.

One solution is DIF (Data Interchange Program) which is evolving into a virtual standard. Many spreadsheets provide utilities to read a DIF file into an active file, or to create a DIF file into a spreadsheet. Increasingly, datacomm capabilities evolve into an intelligent higher-level link transparently supported by the OS and the integrated software offerings.

PC database management (DBMS) packages are another strong (and necessary) trend even if there are no real standards for file formats and data dictionaries (though the Ashton Tate dBase II is a relational DBMS for PCs that can be regarded akin to a standard).

Database management systems have been around for 20 years, but for PCs they still represent an emerging technology. Users are just beginning to realize the potential advantages of tapping the computers information, as the concept of database management is growing.

Even at the mainframe level, many companies which gradually switched from batch-oriented to real-time systems over the last two decades have learned that most programmers and systems analysts are not experienced with DBMS and how to make it work. Most are more familiar with sequential files. Under present-day perspectives, the evolution of such systems will be propelled by relational solutions which are more efficient than the complex, inflexible hierachical and network systems.

Relational systems let nontechnical managers and staff members access a database without specialized skill. Relational approaches help end-users develop databases that contain information relevant to many departments. They permit them to start small and expand their databases slowly. End-users should not have to spend a lot of time figuring out technical details.

This is particularly true for the PC user. His success with personal computing will be in direct proportion to the integrating capability of OS, DBMS, datacomm, electronic mail, spreadsheet, and graphics facilities.

The Macintosh Generation

The first of the new generation of personal WS is Apple's Macintosh. Being a new species, the microsoftware industry is embracing it, anticipating that it will provide another excellent software market.

Macintosh has been no commercial queen, but the solutions it brought forward may become one. From Macintoshes, which are failing, to Xerox Stars, which have failed, we have learned a new end-user discipline. Now we should be looking out for the commercial breakthrough, and this only the right distributor can bring about. But let's examine the *ease of use* technology, the low cost Macintosh helped diffuse.

The Macintosh uses a Motorola 68000 microprocessor (which is a competitive advantage for a single WS); is graphics oriented; features a born mouse and image menu; handles icons; and has no hardware slots.

There are two serial ports (RS 232 or RS 422), and one port for an external Sony three 1/2" floppy with 400 KB. There is also a LAN design orientation. All other extensions can be made through the Applebus for which the PC has a born bus interface unit (BIU).
Applebus is a peripheral device(s) interconnect for small work areas (up to 16 nodes). To reduce the number of commands a user must memorize and type into a computer, *icons* and *popup menus** show users what commands are available to choose from. An icon is a high resolution small graph which identifies for the user the function he is choosing. A wastebasket, a clipboard, a clock, a WP (Macwrite), and a graphic (Macpaint) are examples. A popup menu is a small size menu usually inserted by the machine at the top of the frame to permit choice through cursor positioning. Copy-paste-clear is one such menu; invert-trace-flip-rotate is another.

Bit map, another relatively new term for the end-user, identifies memory association with screen display. The processor can address any point on the screen. This is an expensive approach, and Macintosh has been the first low cost machine at less than $3,000 to support it.

Among the machine specials are an alarm clock, calculator, note pad, and *free form* graphics. With Macpaint, patterns are created, stored and retrieved, and Macwrite permits integrating graphics into a WP menu. The typewriter is emulated on the video and is very easy to use through the mouse.

---

*Apple calls them "pull-down" menus.

The Macpaint and Macwrite facilities are the more interesting if we keep in mind that PC functionality grew out of word processors, calculators and video games. These games can be played both by children and adults; require little instruction; and they reveal themselves: as the user gets better, he discovers them.

The originality of Macpaint is high resolution interactivity. A still picture, no matter how high the resolution, is less satisfying. We need graphics we can interact with. Interactivity must be assisted through prompts, error warning messages, choice possibilities and training aids. The ability to interact with graphics by sliding them around on the screen, stretching, rotating, and shrinking them, is important and satisfying. Many of the classical business graphics fall short in this reference. They do not allow enough interactivity.

For the user, it is important to be able to generate a chart from a set of numbers. It is also important to easily modify numbers and produce a different chart; to change the chart and produce a different set of numbers; to manipulate the chart interactively.

A control panel in Macintosh permits the user to adjust the machine to his pace—and, to a lesser extent, to his choices. It is a good design feature, but if this approach to various capabilities goes too far, then it is no more possible to assure compatibility among different types of equipment.

Emulating typewriter and calculator functions is a current trend. With Macintosh, the classical functional commands are replaced through an array of tiny icons (or pictures). To tell the computer what to do, users point to the appropriate picture on the screen by moving a pointing device called a mouse over a desktop (for example, a file folder represents filing).

Menus are no new subject with computing. They have been extensively promoted with Videotex, but they usually take the entire screen. Now, high resolution videos permit window shades over a limited quadrant of the screen (usually upper left). Also, the popup menu is automatically erased after the choice is made, leaving the rest of the picture unaltered.

Some of these features are found in the Star of Xerox and Apple's Lisa. Macintosh shares icons, windows, and an upward compatibility with Lisa, but at a smaller price.

Visual interplay is the key concept behind both Macintosh and Lisa. Many system designers and human engineering specialists believe pictures are more quickly recognized than words, and Macintosh's bit-mapped graphics make black-and-white pictures quite appealing. The software incorporates both a mouse and bit-mapped graphics. The mouse controls movement of text, data, and images between several applications on the screen. Apple did the graphics shell. (This makes for difficult porting of commodity software applications.)

Furthermore, the operating system is not a commodity offering. Apple has developed a proprietary Resource Manager OS. Since Macintosh is a single WS engine, its operating system and possible developments can be nicely outlined as in Figure 2.1.

Datacomm capabilities include communication with mainframes in the 3278 protocol, as well as emulation of VT 100, VT 52, and TTY. A cluster controller allows up to seven units to be connected to a remote mainframe, and downloading can take place from/to public databases.

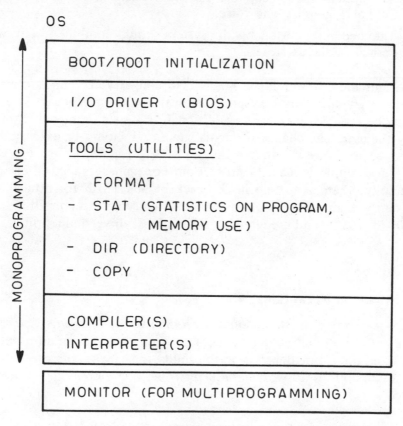

Figure 2.1

Networking is supported through Applebus. The LAN interface is built into Macintosh. Applebus can theoretically carry up to 16 users, but 10 is a more realistic estimate (even if Apple claims 32 nodes). The network runs over a distance of 330 meters, works CSMA/CD, but is relatively slow (230 KBPS).

The goal of Applebus is to tie the machines together, permitting a network level extension of Macintosh with limited machine expandability. As stated, this PC has no slots and features a relatively small central memory.

When it comes to networking, whether for this or other offerings, the following functions are critical:

It should be possible to provide both real-time and deferred (store-and-forward) facilities, with little distinction between the two.

The system should support communications without distinction as to text, graphics and voice.

The media supported by the system should combine in any way desired by the user.

For instance, it should be possible to embed voice annotations in text or graphic images at specific points in a voice message. It must also be feasible to integrate additional, task-specific media required by the user. The change of media supported should be extensible as user demands grow with experience.

An example is security/protection. For managers concerned with security, there is a hole in the back of Macintosh for attaching a security chain. Other options include a carrying case, an OEM-built 300- or 1,200-baud modem, and external disc drive, and a printer.

Software for Networking

WS may work as standalones, or *unnetworked*. In this case they cannot share database resources. This is unwise, as with information systems the future depends on the ability to share databases.

Communicating workstations can be *networked* in either of two ways:

long haul through classical protocols (3270, 2780/3780, TTY, and so on), or local area-oriented through connection to a carrier, typically a coaxial cable or twisted wire.

This carrier can operate *baseband* or *broadband*. A twisted wire, protected twisted wire or coaxial cable featuring one channel, typically digital, between 100 KBPS (kilobits per second) and 10 MBPS (megabits per second) operates in baseband.

Broadband supports a wider bandwidth—up to 450 MHz (Megahertz) under current conditions. This broad range is divided into several channels, which may be of 2.5 MBPS, 10 MBPS or more. The channels may be analog or analog and digital. Protected coaxial cables and optical fibers are usually employed for broadband. Another physical component is the bus interface unit (BIU) which helps connect the WS to the carrier.

What is important in terms of networking workstations is that finally the LAN has come of age. This imposes a need for redirection. Ideally, the network to be chosen should feature:

1. Ease and flexibility in terms of installation and future expansion.
2. Low cost, for instance, less than $100 per node.
3. Fresh, simple protocols requiring less than 2 KB of code on an interface card.
4. The use of VLSI at the nodes.
5. LAN with distributed intelligence beyond the terminal to mainframe image.
6. Solutions geared to the importance and nature of the PC.

The last reference underlines the importance to assure that the protocol and its implementation fits the system environment. Since no off-the-shelf solution can be found for a perfect fit, it is just as vital to engineer the solution after the problem has been identified.

In the background of this statement is that what really counts is the end result. Does the protocol implementation solve the user's problem? Chances are the user's problem is datacomm and databasing. How effectively can this be done?

CSMA/CD. After random timeout, the packet is reissued. If there is a collision, the fallback can be minor. Electrical characteristics include balanced signalling; a standard RS 422 driver and receiver ICs; transformer isolation; passive drops; and FM modulation (hence analog transmission).

What the manufacturer calls "personality module" is a fronted card with two microprocessors sharing RAM (Figure 2.2). This BIU capitalizes on a multitask OS permitting a concurrent sharing of different peripherals.

In the PC resides the Xerox Network Service sequenced packet protocol (XNS/SPP) on 1 KB of ROM. XNS/SPP addresses itself to the transport layer. The system features a lookup function for name service. XNS assures handshake among connected workstations operating at the transport level of ISO/OSI, and contributes to a sharp reduction of the carrier's capacity. (Applied to Ethernet, XNS reduces its capacity by an order of magnitude, to 1 MBPS from 10 MBPS.)

Networks can be interconnected with bridges acting as packet forwarding agents. For telecommunications, the modem is attached to one of the bridges. The transport layer can work in either of the two forms: *data stream* or *transaction handling.*

Provided by the vendor, an Übung simulator serves as a master controls testbed. This helps in configuring nodes from the configuration file, monitoring performance, and gathering statistics. Among the statistics monitored are transmit queue delay, throughput, and errors: CRC, fragmented packets, retries and so on.

The emphasis on datacomm optimization is well-placed. As the last three years of experience show, with online terminals (PC or not) most businesspeople don't want to compute—they want to communicate.

Because it should be able to support a communications-intense environment, the LAN software must include error control, echo suppression, mail transport, and bulk data transfer. It must also be open-ended to new developments, new products, new technologies.

One of the alternatives with Applebus is limited shared data access. This characterized star connections and currently represents the majority of cases in LAN announcements.

Fully shared data access requires program extension—for instance, a database capability. The next step is to fully exploit network potential, beginning with the implementation of electronic mail.

One drawback of Macintosh is its limited central memory.

Supermicros too have drawbacks of their own. One of them, for instance, features:

32 MB of nonformatted disc capacity, but

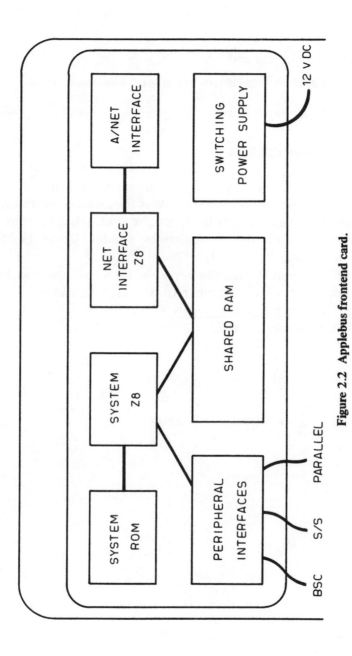

Figure 2.2 Applebus frontend card.

27 MB of formatted disc capacity;

of these were needed

4 MB for a swap area and
11 MB for system files (including menus, libraries),

thus leaving only

12 MB for operating files.

This area represented less than 40% of the stated capacity.

It will be a false assumption to look at the disc volume the vendor states and then compute needs. The right approach is to start from the current and projected requirements, building up to the storage capacity which may be needed.

With this reference, the file server a LAN manages can be the second limitation to the number of WS to be attached. The first limitation, beyond the stated statistics by the vendor, is the channel's text and data transfer capability.

Chapter 3

INTERACTIVE VIDEODISC

Introduction

An Interactive Videodisc (IVD) System is typically microcomputer based and involves multiple storage support: harddisc (HD), laserdisc (LD), videotape or other slide projection, and multiple communications disciplines: Videotex (Vtx), X.25, bisynchronous. As such, it is a complete DB/DC/DP system.

In the sense that it works online to other resources, an interactive videodisc system is a multicommunications aggregate (MCA) available at a reasonable low price for a substantial variety of applications.

Computers and communications are on their way for giving every office the technical capability for engaging in all fields of dynamic image practice. With online to communications networks the PC will become the medium for administrative, marketing, educational, design and artistic purposes.

The laserdisc (videodisc) and its derivatives are becoming more visible as an adjunct to microcomputer use. Depending on its manufacturer, it can store up to 2.5 gigabytes of data on both sides. Access time to any track within a sector is less than 100 ms. Recording can be analog or digital, and silicon has the lifespan necessary for archival storage.

One of the original implementation examples comes from a MIT project (Department of Agriculture) at Aspen, Colorado. Live image taped on V R was catalogued and transfered to Videodisc. With the videodisc machine tied to a PC, a person could walk through Aspen, turn in any direction at any intersection, enter stores, then use the hard disc to make choices.

Several projects are currently involved in multicommunications integration technology, particularly in the United States, Japan and Germany. The object of this effort is to develop an aggregate to handle all needs: data, text, graphs, image, voice and—most importantly—the key issue of documentation. Toshiba, for example, has introduced file 2000 to the market combining harddisc and laserdisc in an aggregate specifically designed to store all company correspondence and related documents. Philips plans the introduction of a computer-based optical disc jukebox which can handle in excess of 50 GB.

All processes within an organization are based on documentation. The classical DP does not answer documentation requirements, and the same is true of CAD/CAM. Text processing with microforms answers them only partially. The real need is for a documentation system on which all other processes can be mapped.

Interactive videodiscs can be used for:

1. Generic file systems providing cross-vendor data compatibility
2. Image and document storage (archival)
3. Backup subsystem to CAD/CAM
4. Computer supported two-way video and audio systems
5. Large information database including the integration of text, data, graphics, image and voice
6. Electronic publishing as well as authoring and editing tools
7. For training purposes in Engineering, Manufacturing, Sales and Service.

There is a growing need for the low cost/large capacity offered by interactive videodiscs. At the same time, augmented by computer power IVD may become the first effective integration of text, data, graphics, image, and voice at the end-user level.

Classical archives typically include data and text references and drawings. Not only should intelligent workstations be able to handle them through user-transparent computer equipment, but also the basis must be documentation with graphics as a support feature.

Five areas are outstanding in terms of implementation:

First, the entire area of office automation (OA) is open to this system.

Archiving is an integral part of OA, from the conversion of paper files to electronic supports to the backup documentation for new processes such as electronic mail. Office automation revamps old office habits through modern technology and integrates many existing supports where archiving plays a vital role.

Second, CAD/CAM-type applications for the archiving of all drawings.

Any company introducing computer-aided design is faced with many preCAD documents. Old drawings should not be redone. This requires some sort of graphical storage which MCA can offer.

Furthermore, there is plenty of opportunity to focus on existing designs using the computer as a high-powered "microscope." In an exhibition in Milan, IBM demonstrated how a PC augmented by laserdisc can be used in the analysis of designs made five centuries ago by Leonardo da Vinci.

Third, integrating graphics and images into DP/WP/CAD for patents, court action, and the transfer of DB from supplier to customer or vice versa.

That is, for *full product documentation,* a process the multicommunications aggregate can effectively support. Archive functions can be limited, such as filing letters and other documents with retrieval through simple keys, or extended. Extended archive functions include the handling of heterogeneous information and retrieval via complex keys. They support the generation of new documents and call for a range of WS communications capabilities.

A key benefit of this new approach to computer-based archiving is in overcoming the old office stuff with the new computer gear. This state of mind often inhibits rational action and is present in the prevailing organizational division between DP and office chores.

Fourth, PCs augmented by laserdisc capability can be effectively used in computer-aided instruction (CAI).

For nearly two decades, CAI was uneconomical because the contact hour with big computers cost more than the teacher. With PC, the ratio reversed itself to the point of costing half the money of the teacher's contact hour, but animation is missing. Programmed laserdiscs can be most effective in this line.

Fifth, marketing activities of all types and in a wide variety of industries.

While computers and word processors have been extensively used in marketing departments for sales statistics and letter writing, their effect was insignificant in direct salesman contact with the clientele. Multicommunications aggregates can change this situation. For example, laserdisc presentations multiply the personal touch of top salesmen by bringing them in contact with populations beyond personal reach.

The Multicommunications Approach

The new dimension of a multifunctional, computer-supported WS is an aggregate of harddisc, interactive videodisc, Videotex and computing functions. Such WS offers the advantages of integrating moving pictures, sound, text/data information, and computer processing.

PCs with harddisc and communications disciplines have already found an expanding implementation. The new unit is the professional, interactive laserdisc utilized as an audiovisual direct access storage device in connection with computers. Images created through and/or managed by PCs can be static for display purposes, such as management graphics, or dynamic. Engineers, scientists, and the artistic community are interested in dynamic images.

Within the multicommunications aggregate (MCA), computer facilities can be used to enhance three technical classes of dynamic image management:

1. The acquisition of image and sound and its storage for retrieval purposes (generally known as production).
2. The processing of stored information to create inference, extrapolation, derivative designs or animation (post-production).
3. The distribution of information to its target address and its display or presentation under a chosen format.

The laserdisc not only stores and reproduces alphanumeric information in a cost/effective manner but also integrates graphics, moving pictures and sound. This reproduction can be shown either as a dynamic picture sequence or as a concatenation of single "info-pages." The computer can make immediately available requested picture and sound sequences, connecting them with information stored in the harddisc or retrieved through communications lines.

The MCA software includes:

A personal computer-supported WS with keyboard, direct access storage, color video as display for still and dynamic pictures, two-channel sound, and frames for Vtx.

A videodisc player or other picture and sound carrier attached to the system (Figure 3.1).

Multimedia software, including an operating system; applications programs; Vtx monitor, other communications routines; and special links for the information elements manipulated by the attached devices, including switching.

More precisely, the operating and communications software needed for MCA contains the following components:

Editing programs for the creation and modification of Btx frames in offline operation.

Administrative routines for storage, manipulation, housekeeping and interlinkage of Vtx frames.

Retrieval software for the request of Vtx frames stored in the PC. (In this respect, the user can use the same functions as with the public Vtx service.)

Communications routines which make possible connections to the Vtx or other external computers.

Special programs for the operation of picture/sound carriers.

Among its advantages, this system offers the user a private Vtx system which allows the same functions as the public videotex service. Thus, a connection to Vtx or an external computer system is done only when needed (for instance, booking a voyage). Telephone charges, problems with unsuccessful connections, and waiting periods are eliminated. At the same time, the user is offered a wider choice of implementations than the one supported by the public service.

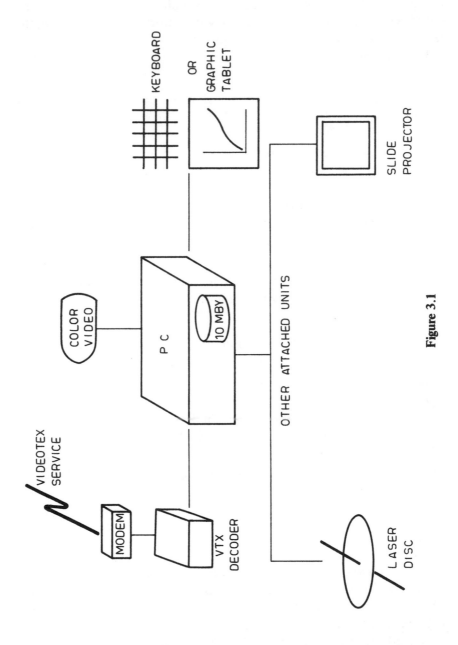

Figure 3.1

The picture and sound material complements the Vtx information, making possible a multimedia approach. Implementations include engineering design, marketing, banking services, and computer-aided instruction.

Let's take as an example a self-service advisory center in a branch office lobby (electronic teller). Through simple commands on the keyboard, the client can obtain a wide range of information: credits, tariffs, savings plans, travel, real estate, etc. via a menu selection capability.

Suppose he chooses real estate. In the now classical Vtx or any text/data presentation, he could obtain simple lines of information in softcopy and, eventually, hardcopy. With the MCA the client is first presented a set of options. Having made his choice, he receives a moving picture of the object which he wants to buy. For the acquisition of this real estate, the Vtx system simultaneously calculates the financing offer, calling the client to input additional data as, for instance, existing capital, desired loan, payment period and so on.

Another applications example is personal training. The person undergoing training can work interactively on the monitor through his study material, seeing in a short film sequence the task, the associated questions and, eventually, the problem solution. Based on his answers, the participant is guided through the study material. Correct answers lead him to the next step. Depending on their seriousness, wrong answers branch back to past learning sequences.

This has been the classical approach with CAI. What is new is that a major part of the textual presentation has been replaced by role-playing. Actors present alternative scenarios from which the participant must choose, and he can replay this dynamic lesson as often as he wishes.

For instance, one videodisc microcomputer application is the interactive training for learning to use the IBM PC. Interactive Research has created a program that uses a Sony or Pioneer laserdisc player joined to an IBM PC. This program permits the new computer user to learn to operate the computer and some specific applications by following very clear pictorial directions on a color video screen. We can expect to see more videodisc training materials as the laserdisc microcomputer interface comes into widespread use.

Quite importantly, the layout of the learning steps and picture sequences can be different from one repetition to another, thus allowing different viewpoints. The computer-supported system allows the tie-up of dialogs into a complete study program.

Other applications work in a similar manner. These may involve the presentation of travel plans and transport/hotel reservations; client-handling procedures including the analysis of client requests; management presentation from the preparation of charts and graphs to archiving sequences; and the support of dynamic group presentations.

Logical Components of a Multicommunications System

The creation of software for a MCA poses new demands on project and systems management. Systems analysts and software specialists must collaborate in designing interactive, audiovisual computer programs and controls implementation. Systems programming skill is necessary to integrate the logical components of a multicommunications aggregate:

control programs,

multimicroprocessor architectures,

different types of database engines,

videodisc adjuncts to local databases,

interfaces for databasing and datacomm,

graphics workstations, and

multiple interrupt capabilities.

The first task of the software specialist in assuring the proper multi-interrupt control programs is to review problem specifications to properly define the interactivity scenarios which will involve two major parts—SW/HW system design and a system view of end-usage requirements (Figure 3.2).

The next step is the integration of specifications and support tools involving multimedia software and the incorporation of image and sound. This task typically uses existing components and is followed by implementation and fine-tuning.

With MCA, the system analysts and software specialists should be joined by a dialog advisor who works on interactivity analysis and dialog tuning. In this latter phase, the coordination between lines of computer code and videotakes is optimized.

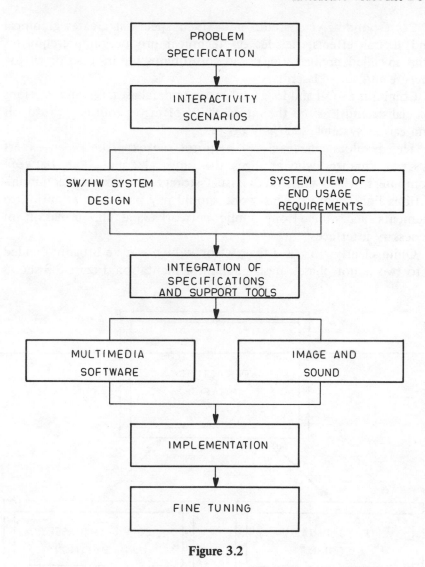

Figure 3.2

The scenario writer collaborates with the systems analysts within the interdisciplinary teams. The dialog specialist works both as a scenario developer and as a consultant in analyzing usage needs; he also creates specifications for the design of component computer programs, of videotakes (of moving picture scenes), and other information elements.

Correspondingly, a studio and video specialist creates graphical and digital effects; decides on technical production prerequisites (the so-called premastering); and coordinates the production of the picture and sound laserdiscs.

Combining local and long haul access to databases, communications specialists must assure the interactivity of driver routines, protocols and carrier systems, such as Videotex.

The development team also requires the expertise of an expert systems engineer who arranges the physical connections between computers, video units, audiovisual storage devices, and communications line adaptors. This work should pay particular attention to elements accessible from public networks and the provision of necessary interfaces.

Quite clearly, this is a team effort which can be broadly divided into two major phases: design and implementation. Figure 3.3 shows

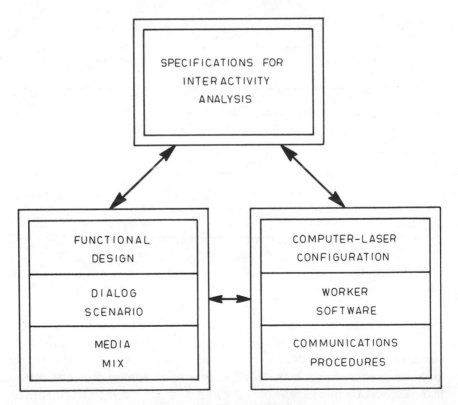

Figure 3.3 Phase 1: Design.

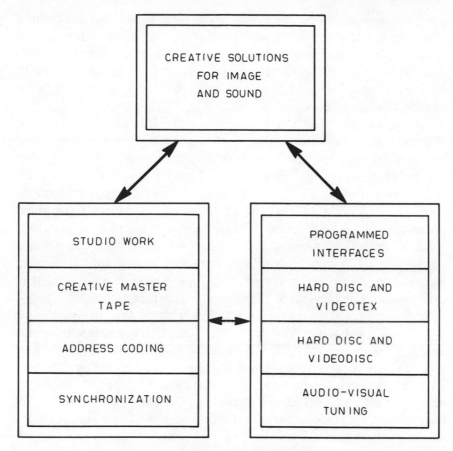

Figure 3.4 Phase 2: Implementation.

the three logical parts of the design task. Each exercises considerable influence on the others, forcing reevaluations and modifications to the specs.

Some of the design considerations filter into the implementation phase (Figure 3.4). This is, for instance, happening with the creative solutions for image and sound. Here again there are three highly interconnected component parts.

One of the key duties of the systems engineer is—together with the end-user—to study the choice between analog and digital recording media on laserdisc. No a priori solutions should exist on this subject. Decisions should be taken after careful study of implementation requirements. For example, in a CAD/CAM environment, analog recording on laserdisc may make feasible the conversion of a large library of existing drawings to an online mode. While several research groups today work on digitizing drawings, most implementation work rests on optical scanners. (Some projects work with DIN A0 size drawings, but the majority use DIN A3 and DIN A4 (8 1/2x11 inches).)

Hence, the answer to the question, "Should an analog or digital approach be used?" is a matter of applications requirements and available technology. Much depends on the way we wish to present the information to the computer and on the available conversion procedures. (Graphical data and images can be processed in analog form or are coded into digital for storage and decoded for video presentation. A way to avoid this is through the use of laserdiscs.)

Thus, optical memory discs are part of the database processor engine storing not only text and data but also graphics, moving images and voice. Such systems must be provided with agile user interfaces and be capable of handling user commands.

While optical disc drives are read-only, the new generation of laserdiscs is read/write. This leads to a total functional duality—hard disc for read/write of text and data and laserdisc for read/write of graphics, images and voice. Local area networks can nicely integrate with and support this system. For instance, the Technical University of Darmstadt has worked out a solution involving an Ethernet LAN augmented by a graphics server on which each WS has its microfiles.

System Manager, Foreman, Worker

The MCA has a mission and a systems structure. We have seen the mission requirements, and now we will examine the functional system overview leading to the structure of the aggregate. The diagram in Figure 3.5 distinguishes between the user (man or program) and the logical blocks constituting the MCA.

1. The user level.

The user level must be provided with the appropriate interface for inquiring, retrieving, and storing data, and for issuing appropriate commands to the MCA manager. Typically, inquiry commands will

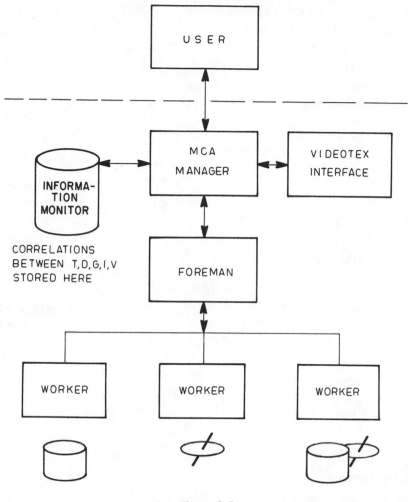

Figure 3.5

involve lists of keywords, lists of documents and subdocuments, and the like. The user must also have the possibility of defining conjunctions between two or more commands (logical and, or, not). This calls for the implementation of a user-friendly very high level language.

Retrieval commands can be of two kinds: get structure of document and get data of document/subdocument. Store commands are necessary to update previously stored information, adding new IE, and creating new documents.

Typically, when using an update command, the user first has to do a retrieval. He can subsequently create documents/subdocuments, add to subdocuments, update IE or the structure of a document, update keywords, and so on.

2. MCA manager.

This has three purposes: handling requests posed by the user; communicating with the monitor of the information resource (eventually a DBMS); and running the *foreman* or foremen in its direct dependence.

In other words, the MCA manager is receiving and queueing user orders; scheduling and issuing internal requests and associated instructions; receiving command data; and generating answers at the user level. Two levels of reference should be specified: microcomputer or other computer equipment, and the local area network (LAN) environment.

At the level of the MCA manager may be added other logical components, such as a videotex interface. This interface would have the dual function of presenting a Vtx menu and of connecting to the coder/decoder for public line communications.

In a self-standing computer device, the MCA manager is a routine resident in central memory—though it may also occupy the full resources of an attached device. In a LAN, the MCA manager is a server whose main task is protocol handling for the desired interconnection between the database server and the user workstation(s).

When receiving a user command, the MCA manager decides whether it will be stored before the execution or executed at once. Depending on the kind of command, it issues the necessary internal system requests to the information monitor and/or the foreman. During the final steps of handling a user request, it receives both user data and status reports, generating an answer at the user level.

3. The information monitor.

The role of the information monitor closely resembles a knowledgebank in an expert system. It contains problems and relations, providing linkages between text, data, graphics, moving images and voice contained in the database. The information elements constituting this knowledgebank could be run like any IE through a DBMS. IE and commands must be protected from SW/HW failures, and should, therefore, be saved periodically.

More specifically, the information monitor handles commands of the MCA manager, creates entries of new documents, updates entries of documents, retrieves locations of documents in a user-indexed manner (via keywords), retrieves the structure of documents, and assures correlations.

Database routines should execute the saving procedures automatically each time the optical disc is removed from its drive. Other housekeeping chores are necessary as the size of the laserdisc memory grows and the hard disc updates become more frequent.

4. The foreman.

The foreman controls the workers. Its mission is to receive and queue internal system commands from the information monitor subsystem and the MCA manager. It schedules the functions to be performed and issues appropriate instructions to the designated workers.

The mission of the foreman is closely related to that of the workers, who are specialized. The foreman

receives internal system commands,

queues these commands for execution,

schedules worker functions,

issues commands to workers,

combines worker responses into single answer T, D, G, I, V, and

sends data bottom-up to the requesting authority.

Coordination routines are also necessary as the foreman supervises a number of workers whose functionality is that of a driver for basic peripheral interfaces (Figure 3.6).

5. The workers.

The worker(s) update the user IE, combine updates with original information, execute tasks such as window processing and grid conversion, encode and decode image data, and interface with the controllers of the laserdiscs.

At the Interactive Videodisc project of the Technical University of Darmstadt, workers are accessed in parallel and specialized by function: text, data, graphics, image. Voice capabilities can be added.

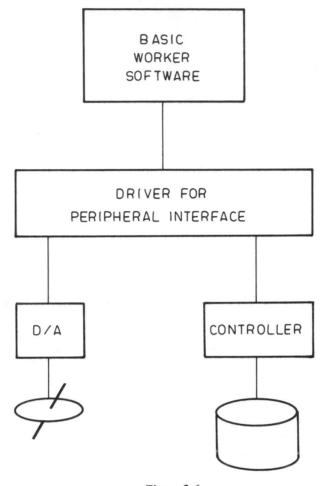

Figure 3.6

A physical configuration is presented in Figure 3.7 through a LAN solution. The information monitor is a file server. The datacomm server connects to public network(s), for instance, Videotex and/or packet switching. Workers "o" to "n" are attached to the system running hard discs and optical discs.

A careful study should be done to reduce I/O transfer time and, at the worker level, to minimize head positioning. Other parameters depend on hardware technology. Redundant positioning for the optical disc can be avoided if the queries in the buffer are sorted.

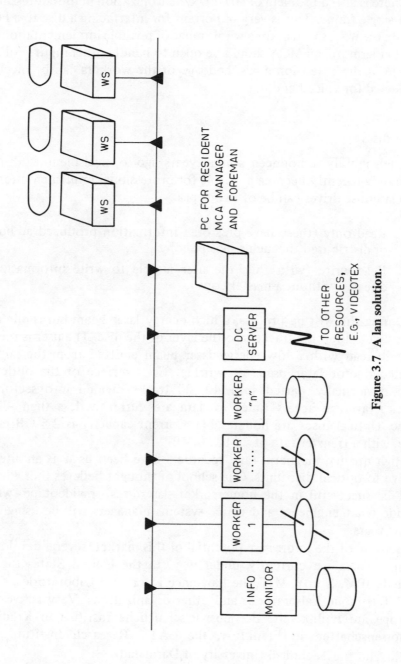

Figure 3.7 A lan solution.

There is also a problem of HD/LD synchronization in the addressing of a single frame. This is very important for interfacing a disc to a PC within the WS, as well as for a whole range of possible implementations.

Furthermore, an MCA should be open to handle other input. Voice is one of the extension goals, and one of the workers can be nicely projected for voice handling.

Laserdiscs

Though initally announced several years ago, optical memory discs have only recently become available for professional implementation. The laserdisc drives can be of two types:

1. Read only (these have prestored information produced ad hoc or distributed through a master copy).
2. Read/write (with this, the user is able to write information directly without a master copy).

During the writing process, a high energy laser beam burns miniature holes along the tracks into the layer of the disc. The user is then able to read with a low energy laser beam emitted from the same semiconductor laser used for writing. Each surface of the optical disc is normally parted into 40,000 tracks divided into sectors. Typical average access times to data are currently less than 400 msec. Optical discs are nonerasable. Current capacity is 2.5 GB per disc, with a transfer rate of up to 20 MBPS.

High quality magnetic tape recorders have been used as an alternative to optical disc-units. One school of thought believes that what will be successful in the homemarket—laserdiscs or videotape—will decide what engineers and office systems managers will be using in a few years.

Because of the impressive potential of this market, several development efforts are currently under way. In the United States these include IBM, Xerox, MIT, the Lawrence Livermore Laboratories, the Bell Telephone Laboratories and other organizations. Very active in Europe are Philips, the Betriebswirtschaftliche Institut fur Kreditgenossenschaften in Frankfurt, the CATV Research Institute in Berlin, and the Technical University of Darmstadt.

Chapter 4

ECONOMICALLY JUSTIFYING THE WORKSTATION

Introduction

Many industrial and financial institutions are in the process of evaluating the advisability of a distributed information system (DIS) based on PCs and LAN. The aim of this solution is to bring computer power to every desk.

Alternatives are being considered and, sometimes, the old way is retained not because of any solid technical and economic justification but because of routine and resistance to change. That's exactly what should *not* be done. The adoption of a new technology helps reduce costs, keeping the company competitive.

As an example, Apple IIe reduced its component count from 110 to 31 by replacing many chips wired into printed circuit boards (PCB) with two LSI custom chips. The cost of such custom chips might be equal to or higher than the cost of the standard chips they replace when their fixed engineering cost is figured in, but they make possible significant savings in:

assembling circuit boards,

simplifying many aspects of the system's design and/or construction, and

increasing system reliability.

Resolving technical and economic problems has become the goal of companies promoting the use of high technology. As a matter of principle, successful firms pay more attention to development than to failures. Successful management innovates in response to market needs and involves end-users in the development of the innovation.

The case studies included in this text come from experience with industrial and financial organizations. To demonstrate the procedural steps, a serious system design should be implemented. To make the profit picture more evident, a discussion on the background factors to a PC/LAN solution is included.

A Banking Environment

The Foreign Operations department of a main branch office employs 36 persons for a Foreign Trade and Money Exchange. This group includes the manager, four section heads, six secretaries, six front desk professionals, 18 back office professionals, and a messanger.

Typical applications are:

1. Relations with the client base (manager and section heads, part time)
2. Prospecting (two of the 18 back office professionals)
3. Clearance for import
4. Associated currency calculations (import)
5. Conversion to local currency
6. Issue of payment orders to foreign correspondents/debit of client account (after converting to local currency)
7. Clearance for export
8. Associated currency calculations (export)
9. Issue of credit notes to clients/debit of correspondent account (after converting to local currency)
10. Letters of credit
11. Client information debit/credit
12. Answer of queries by clients on state of order processing
13. Idem for corresponding banks (by manager)
14. Transactions and payments of all types (other than those described)
15. Balancing of accounts
16. General Ledger/Forex
17. Daily reporting to government authorities: import/export, by currency, type of merchandise, origin/destination
18. Upkeep of the foreign exchange database as legally required

19. Management statistics by client, section, type of operation, correspondent, country, product, type of money
20. Calculation of commissions
21. Upkeep of client files
22. Datacomm to central operations (current accounts, etc.) for updating
23. Handling of electronic mail with headquarters
24. Handling of telex communications with clients, banks and SWIFT (at HQ)
25. Handling of correspondence (at HQ)
26. Documentation of all sorts
27. Miscellaneous items regarding daily business.

These applications consume 100% of the stated employees' time—and there are outstanding demands for an increase in personnel. Operations are made in phases:

Clearance is done by the professional at his desk, along with annotations.

After the official exchange rates are communicated (midday), the same person proceeds with data input offline on the terminal.

Data is stored on floppies and sent online to the computer center.

Client correspondence is made by typewriter (idem for corresponding banks), subsequent to the operational system but independent of it.

Money changes are first handled on a calculator, then a receipt is made.

The currently available equipment includes 23 phones. The manager, section heads, and secretaries each have a phone. Two professionals share one phone. The department has eight online/offline terminals used intermittently off-desk by the 24 professionals (feeding through public lines to a mainframe). There are also 30 typewriters for secretaries and professionals; 32 calculators; three electronic mail terminals; and two telex machines. Manual files are kept, while some 50 different forms are being used due to lack of standardization.

A system study has the objective of improving the current situation. Firstly, the procedural issues were examined and a standardization effort for forms and documentation was enacted. The goal was to reduce paperwork by 80% within the perspective of office automation.

Six alternatives were considered within the framework of four system solutions:

Solution 1 looked after the substitution conventional equipment (typewriters, calculators, nonintelligent terminals) by similar but modern units.

The aim of this evaluation was to improve cost/effectiveness on an "as is" basis and to serve as a point of reference. Technically, this presented no innovation. The costs are contained, and the benefits even more so.

Solution 2 took the approach of changing from a centralized real-time option to locally installed minis to support less then five to six second response times.

Two options fit within this approach. One gives one minicomputer-based, nonintelligent terminal to each of the department's 35 employees. The other does so for only the managers and secretaries, while giving one terminal per two professional employees—a total of 23.

Solutions 3 and 4 adopt the PC and LAN approach. The former puts a PC under every desk; the latter gives machines to only 23 people.

Furthermore, with Solution 3 there are two alternatives. The more expensive one incorporates a 10 MB hard disc (HD) per PC over and above the 40 MB file server of the LAN. The other, more economical alternative does away with the HD. Both alternatives support 35 WS on two LAN, but the more expensive one has 512 KB and 10 MB, whereas the other has 256 KB and floppies.

A basic assumption of the systems study focused on productivity gains. These were evaluated at 20% for Solution 3 only, with the following possible savings:

Now	Will Be	Economy of
1 manager	1.2	–
4 section heads	4.8	1
6 secretaries	7.2	1
24 professionals	28.8	5

About 7 persons

Different vendor sources were examined for Solutions 3 and 4. Three were retained on the basis of technical potential. This was followed by a financial evaluation. As seen in Figure 4.1, supplier B is definitely very expensive and out of range. As a result, he has been dropped. The other two (suppliers C and E) are price-wise quite comparable.

Comparing the PC/LAN vs. minicomputer solutions (3 and 4 vs. 2), we see that the cost per intelligent WS vs. the nonintelligent one stands at about:

$6,200 vs. $16,700 for each of the 23 WS and
$6,600 vs. $17,000 for each of the 35 WS.*

This economic evaluation suggests that the minicomputer solution with its "stupid" terminals is many times more expensive than PC/LAN which brings programmable workstations to every desk. Since the maxi-to-mini cost ratio per supported terminals hovers around 3.0 to 3.2—the difference of the mainframe to PC/LAN is roughly 8:1—we see that personal computing gives much better service.

This being factually documented, the system designers' attention once again focused on the key choices. The alternatives considered were one WS per person and one WS per "n" persons (two in this case). A vote taken between system specialists went in favor of the former.

Then came the fine-tuning of the systems solution and its economic background. Working with supplier C's offer, the analysts first examined the wisdom of a slightly smaller configuration in WS hardware:

*At the time this study was made.

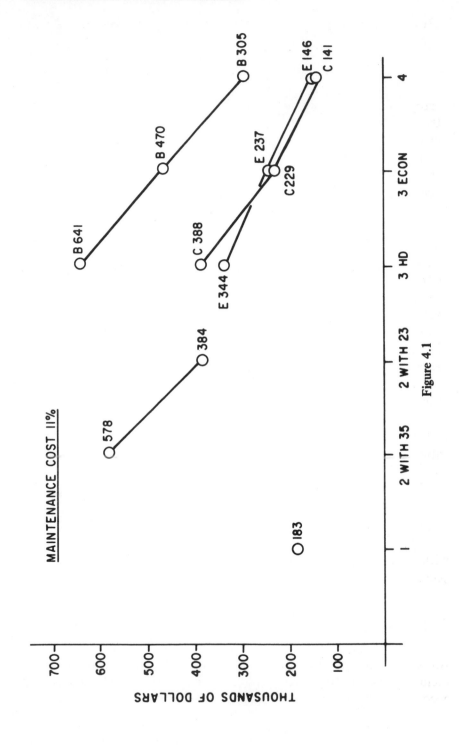

Figure 4.1

If the five managers and 10 professionals have no printer	$18,000
If 256 KB is enough	35,000
Sum	$53,000

Figure 4.2 presents the result. For both Solution 3 alternatives, at 20% higher productivity, seven posts can be eliminated (at $8,200 per post and, say, three printers).

In the process of fine-tuning, the need was, however, highlighted for added hardware. For one network (Solution 4), one streamer was necessary at about $18,000 as well as two WS backups ($16,400), hence a total expense of $34,400. For two networks (both Solution 3 alternatives), two streamers, three backups and a bridge. Hence, $36,000 plus $24,600 plus $4,900 equals $65,500.

Figure 4.3 demonstrates the increase in cost for the different alternatives due to reliability considerations. Part of this expense was compensated by a 10% discount by the supplier for a sale of over 20 units.

Let's look now at the economical aspects of this proposition. We have spoken of eliminating seven persons. The company in reference has 40 sales offices spread over a wide geographic area divided into four regions. Each regional office coordinates eight to 12 local offices, interfacing between the local sales office and headquarters.

The sales offices and regions communicate among themselves, the factories, and headquarters through telex and phone calls. Communication with clients and prospects is through phone, letters, and telex. On the average, the sales office employs five salespeople; the range is three to 10. Each sales office has a manager with a small warehouse for local deliveries (individuals, retailers) typically employing two or three persons.

Each region has a manager and six or seven people mainly occupied with coordinating the commercial network and handling large accounts, and about 10 professionals whose work is custom engineering (systems) design for one of the company's product lines.

Both at the sales offices and regions, the salespeople need to consult inventory cards to confirm product availability—and this is done through a manual search while the salesperson is on the phone. All executed customer orders are billed centrally (average delay including data entry is 10 to 12 days). Follow-up on client accounts, account payments, prospecting and so on is done at the sales office

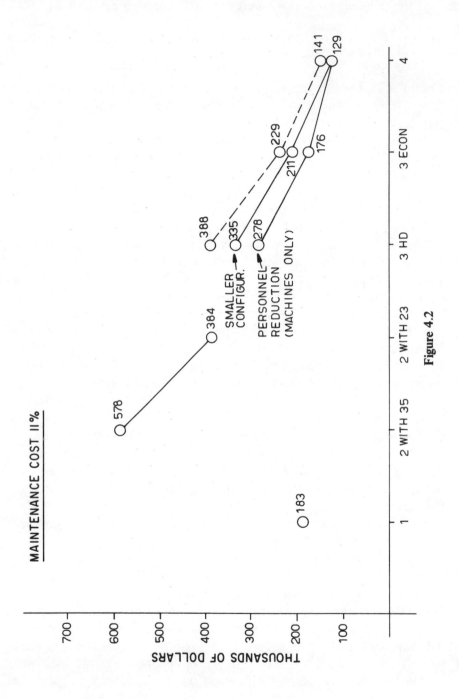

Figure 4.2

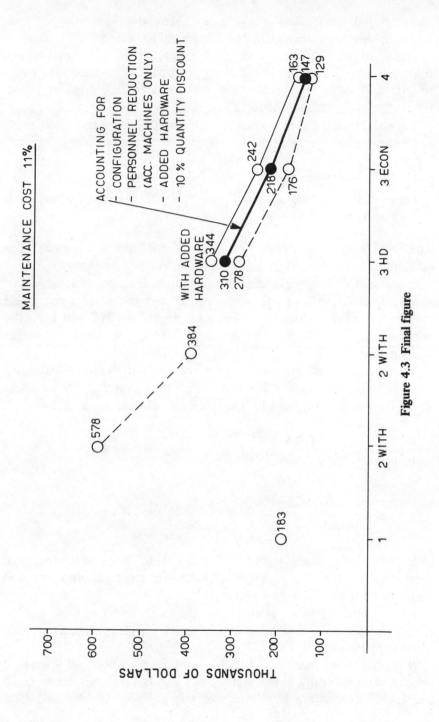

Figure 4.3 Final figure

and regional levels. The object is to automate both using PC and LAN (the latter where justified) with a local database.

Applications should include online inquiry on inventory status; sales confirmation; online data entry; gateway(s) to clients; gateway to HQ and factories; production inquiries; local billing; and electronic mail substituting for telex.

Let's start with the fundamentals. One manager and five salespeople can have:

On the basis of one salesman, one PC per 6 WS

On the basis of two salesmen, one PC (with the manger having his own unit) per 4 WS.

The local warehouse needs two WS, and with the 1:1 solution this adds up to eight WS plus one file server (FS) and one gateway.

Since sale office operations are not complex, the WS can be of low cost. It is sufficient that it be able to handle order entry and inventory update. Video, 256 KB, and printer per WS will keep the cost around $3,000. To this must be added the joint file server and gateway.

Because all salesmen access the same files, it makes no sense to provide microfiles at the WS level. To dimension the FS we must know the number of items in inventory for all four product lines.

A. White	300–400
B. Brown	200–300
C. Lamps	1,000–1,500
D. Specials	2,000–2,500
	3,500–4,700

Say an average if 4,000; at 1,000 bytes each, they call for four MB. That's only a fraction of a typical LAN file server. More space will be needed for the billing operation.

Applications software is an important issue, and the concept is to generalize the WS supports for all sales offices throughout the company operations.

If no hard disc is used at the WS level for salesmen and inventory people, with HD only at the manager's level, the cost will be $65,000 per LAN—including a bus interface unit, a FS of 80 MB, and gateways. This is the cost reflected in the proposal of Vendor E. The cost for Vendor C is $91,000 per sales office.

We said that the commercial network has 40 sales offices and four regional offices. Considering them to have nearly equal needs—for an order of magnitude evaluation*—the total cost including basic software and applications packages stands at:

supplier E $2,860,000
supplier C $4,000,000

For over 100 units, Vendor E offers a 30% price reduction. Hence, the investment stands at $1,900,000.

Let's now examine savings from direct billing. The distributed commercial network accounts for over 60% of total business. (The balance is engineering specials and direct sales from HQ.) $1.5 billion per year corresponds to these operations. At 300 days per year, this amounts to $5,000,000 per day. With distributed billing, the company calculated to obtain a 10-day difference in value—or $50,000,000 per year. With the prevailing 12% interest paid to banks, this amounts to $60,000,000 per year.

If management can reduce the current 12 days of delay to 2 days, then it can pay for the whole system in 4 months. Six months may be more plausible, accounting for reorganization, systems study, implementation, introduction of new forms, training and "babysitting."

The Factory Environment

The company has 10 factories; four belong to Division A, three to Division B, two to Division C and one to Division D. Each factory has a warehouse for its own products and acts as a depot for the products of the other divisions. For about a dozen years, these factories have employed minicomputers. Mainframes are at headquarters, along with CAD/CAM.

Manufacturing Operations wants to modernize factory applications which today include:

---

*Without accounting for CAD/CAM at the regional level. This will be examined in the following section.

1. Production planning and control
2. Production statistics
3. Quality control statistics
4. Raw materials
5. In-process inventories
6. Ready goods in warehouse/other company factories
7. Expediting (out of inventories to small warehouses, wholesalers, retailers, etc.)
8. Technical operations (maintenance, new constructions)
9. Merits and demerits (labor incentives)
10. Personnel (salaries, wages)
11. Analytic accounting (cost control)
12. General accounting
13. Various administrative duties
14. Management information.

Items 1, 2, 4, 6, 8 and partly 14 are currently on the mini. Each of the present-day installations has six nonintelligent terminals. At night, it does batch work.

A system analysis established that the "typical" factory will require 38 WS on the production floor, in the warehouse, in the staff departments, and for administrative/management purposes. Here were three alternatives:

1. If the minicomputer line was followed, six minus would be required for response time reasons, with tough interconnection problems to be resolved.
2. A mixed solution would involve minis and PCs (at the upper price range level).
3. Two LAN could easily divide the 38 WS and maintain a low response times.

Alternative 1 called for much more important expenditures while at the same time being much less reliable.

Alternative 2 gave slightly better results, but generally was not satisfactory. While the original idea was that the old software could be saved (hence, one mini per factory), a more detailed study demonstrated that everything had to be done again.

Alternative 3 was chosen. Due to the fact that at most WS there was both a specialized and a generalized type of work, it was decided to chose PCs with hard discs (11 MB) at a cost of $7,000 per unit.

Both solutions E and C were evaluated. The WS cost was practically the same for both; the same is true of software. There was a minor difference in the cost of servers and BIU:

Supplier E: $383,000 per typical factory—$3,830,000 for total network.

Supplier C: $427,000 per typical factory—$4,270,000 for total network.

Supplier E won the competition for three reasons:

1. Its file server solution was much more elegant than that of supplier C.
2. It presented a compatibility to the commercial network.
3. The vendor offered a 30% reduction as contrasted to the 20% of supplier C for the 380 WS plus supporting gear.

This brought the cost of the total plant automation to $2,280,000. Improved production planning, better inventory control (and, therefore, a reduction in spares and assemblies), more effective administrative controls and efficient communications were the key benefits from this phase of factory automation.

In the original implementation which took place in the 1970s, manufacturing engineering was not on the minicomputer. Many records and design blueprints remained manual. Management thus decided to introduce CAD/CAM and to link this equipment to the central resources. For one of the factories, the link was also to take place toward the regional engineering groups.

The low-cost 32-bit-based new generation of CAD/CAM units were chosen: one per factory, two per regional office, and two at HQ as interfaces to the already established CAD/CAM implementation.

For a 20-unit order at a total cost of $300,000, the vendor offered a 10% discount. At each distributed location the CAD/CAM equipment was attached to the LAN. This implementation accentuated the benefits derived from the factory automation.

Chapter 5

PROJECTING THE WORKSTATION

Introduction

The first basic thing to realize in a WS project is that the new equipment will present new functionality and replace units already in existence. During the last 20 years, office functions have been performed by a variety of machines which must now be integrated into the WS.

Electric typewriters, filing cabinets, microforms, calculators, timesharing terminals, telephone sets, telex equipment, copiers and telecopiers, facsimile, videotex units, and even standalone PCs are examples of supports which have assisted office functions. What is more, the people employing such machines have adapted to them.

The new office system *cannot* afford to forget about these realities. It must account for them; reflect on the replacement of diverse and incompatible units we now employ through more agile, programmable media; integrate their functionality into one properly designed WS; and, above all, assure the interfaces to the human user.

Interfaces to the end-user fall into two large categories: those nearby permitting text/data entry along with storage and presentation, and the links to further-out services needed to perform one's own functions and contribute to those of others. Such linkages are assured through online communications, making the use of datacomm protocols an issue of great importance.

Furthermore, both nearby and further-out solutions should be subject to system integration. This makes file compatibility a prime requirement, followed by the appropriate service scheduling and the expediting of local files to desired locations.

So, projecting a WS is both a local and a system activity. In the latter case the system architect is required to design the divisional assignments between WS; the local database; the files in that database; semaphores to files; memo-posting procedures; electronic mail capabilities; local area networking; long haul datacomm; connections between the local database and the company's mainframe(s); local consistency in update; and global consistency. Elegant and effective solutions depend on user *and* vendor cooperation.

The User Interface

For years, individuals have been served online through nonintelligent terminals (or by micros in a terminal emulation mode) accessing a central or regional resource. To integrate these lower level devices with those in the center of the organization, standard communication protocols and data definitions have been worked out.

Today, intelligent workstations represent the most dynamic part of our field. They feature relatively low prices, and are fast developing toward a universal adoption. Yet, there are issues which have not yet been resolved.

This is particularly true of input media. Until recently, the user had to sit at the computer keyboard typing arcane and hard-to-remember commands to make his computer work.

Nonintelligent terminals provide only a limited solution to the end-user's computing needs. They are not the panacea that they may have appeared to be. With the advent of personnel computing power at the WS level, emphasis on information systems has been shifting from central and/or mini-based to fully distributed computer resources.

Communicating office machines, point of sales (POS) equipment, and automatic tellers are terminals. Since 1970 their growth in terms of installations has been fantastic. Terminals are located at remote sites: banks, telephone companies, merchandizing firms, airlines, manufacturers, oil companies, and government institutions head this list.

Yet, while the time of the nonintelligent terminal is past, it has also left a legacy imposing constraints. Even a PC is not free of them; the user has to change floppies every time he wants to change from one job to another. What is more, information may have to be typed in again if he needs to use it in another procedure.

Though integrated software aims to correct this flaw, the fact remains that the user must employ some sort of text/data entry interface which has not yet been optimized for large scale implementation. Some alternatives are presented in Figure 5.1.

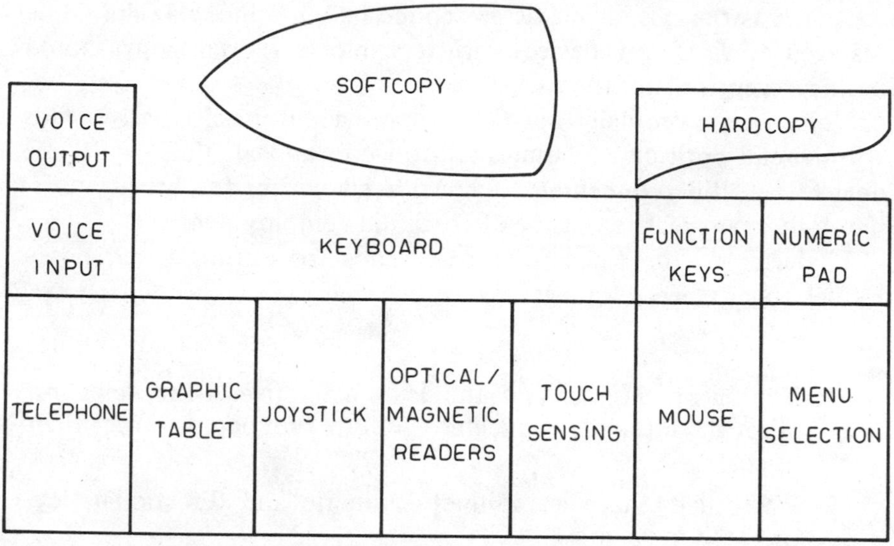

VOICE OUTPUT	SOFTCOPY					HARDCOPY	
VOICE INPUT	KEYBOARD					FUNCTION KEYS	NUMERIC PAD
TELEPHONE	GRAPHIC TABLET	JOYSTICK	OPTICAL/ MAGNETIC READERS	TOUCH SENSING	MOUSE		MENU SELECTION

Figure 5.1 An Integrated WS.

For output, presentations are best—preferably color with graphics capability. Video units come in different

technologies (refresher, raster, gas panel)
sizes (9″, 12″, 13″, 15″, 19″)
number of columns/rows (40x24, 80x24, 80x48, 80x25, 132x24)*
resolutions measured in thousands of pixels: 128, 256, 512, 1024
Colors or presentation (2, 4, 7, 64, more).

Some offerings present the possibility of choosing 4,000 different colors out of a total population of 32,000. Others give the possibility of changing the number of supported lines and columns and the pixel per character. For instance, IBM's 3290 flat panel can have 9,920 characters of 5x8 in 62 lines and 150 columns (split screen) or 5,300 characters of 7x10 in a 52-line and 106 characters-per-line presentation. Many video offerings feature split screen capability, handle windows, and make feasible touch sensing. Video presentation is often referred to as *softcopy*.

---

*Often in a 25 line video, the twenty-fifth line is reserved for diagnostic and other messages.

As far as the output media are concerned, a minor role should be reserved to *hardcopy* devices (printers, plotters). Hardcopy should be the exception, not the rule.

Voice may eventually become a popular output alternative. This will depend both on economics and on user appeal. Voice synthesis devices are still rudimentary if considered within the broad implementation perspective outside of voice mail employment.

If these are the three principal means for output, input possibilities cover a broader range:

1. The most classical and the least attractive is the *keyboard* (though infrared connected remote keyboards have their appeal).

2. WS usually have an adjunct, numeric and directional key-oriented *keypad*.

3. Programmed functions can be called through *function keys*.

4. *Voice input* is a distinct possibility, either at the level of functional calls or for structured text/data entry.

5. A *Graphic tablet* can provide fast first class capabilities from computer-aided design to foreign exchange operations.

6. The *mouse*, particularly a device equipped with functional keys, is a recent favorite.

7. *Track balls* are an alternative and have been used in CAD environments.

8. *Joysticks* currently have limited applications in offices, other than as wireless infrared connections to WS for cursor positioning.

9. *Touch sensing* screens are an alternative combined with logical support such as menu selection.

10. *Optical* and/or *magnetic readers* can be used to facilitate the input of standard data.

11. The mouse, track ball, joystick, touch sensing screens, and other means are pointing devices permitting cursor positioning. This leads to *menu selection*.

An experiment made by Nixdorf at the 1985 Hanover Fair, in Germany, demonstrated that the No. 1 choice by a sample of 2,000 users who understood an appropriately defined experiment, has been the hand actuated mouse. The keyboard ended next to the last position in a classification which involved seven alternatives. In the second position was the graphic tablet (business applications).

Though menu selection can be seen as the logical understructure necessary for a given physical implementation, it is also a self-standing solution. At a 1984 conference in Washington, D.C., users preferred menu selection through a keypad with a keyboard for text/data entry rather than mouses so massively introduced during 1983 by many vendors. Users, in fact, expressed great doubt for the real service some of the enumerated alternatives really present.

In this sense, menu selection should be seen not as a generalized approach but as *the specialized interface by profession for embedded applications.*

In the same conference, AT&T presented three workbench machines following the embedded applications concept. Another application that attracted attention concerned a legal office in New York City where 300 lawyers worked through PCs with an embedded applications approach.

Contrasted to this solution, generalized pointing devices aim to answer the requirements of a broader user population. The mouse and touch screen are examples.

The mouse is a handheld device that slides along a desk. It has one to three functional microswitches, two perpendicular wheels, and a potentiometer, and is connected to the PC through a physical RS 232 connection of 300 or 1,200 baud. As the mouse moves, the cursor on the screen moves accordingly. A user can point to much smaller objects with a mouse than with a finger, and the screen is not obscured. Drawbacks are that a clear space is needed next to the computer, and using a mouse requires leaving the keyboard.

The first electronic mouse was developed at Stanford Research Institute in the mid-1960s. Xerox sold the first product with some of these features in the Star computer system in 1981, and Apple Computer further refined those ideas in its Lisa in early 1983.

In late 1983, IBM introduced a desktop machine that gives windowing capabilities to corporate clients communicating with large mainframe computers. That same year, Hewlett-Packard made a screen-sensitive entry by lining the video with emitters and detectors of infrared light so that the front of the screen is crossed by an invisible grid of beams. Another technique is to coat the screen with a transparent membrane that contains wires or conductive coating so that pressing the screen completes a circuit at a particular point.

Pointing can be a more natural way of using a computer than typing commands. However, those who do word processing or financial calculations on a spreadsheet have to type the text or numbers anyway and might find it bothersome to leave the keyboard to touch the screen occasionally. That is especially true as they gain experience. Frequent users would rather type a few characters rather than reach up and touch the screen and come down again. There are other drawbacks as well. The pointing hand obscures the text, and the finger is too bulky to pinpoint single letters. Also, arms become weary and screens get dirty.

Touch screens are finding employment where the computer is used for short periods by novices, such as the information displays at Walt Disney's Epcot Center in Florida. They may be useful for educational purposes, especially in work with young children. Control Data's Plato computerized education system was a pioneer in touch screen use. They also allow people in high-stress situations to go through a sequence of actions quickly without taking their eyes off the screen. At the American Stock Exchange, a specialist can execute a trade by touching the order as it comes up on the screen.

Eventually, the success of the mouse or of touch screens will largely depend on the supporting software. Such support should definitely include a multiwindow manager to

scroll up, down, left, right

command windows: insert, delete, shrink, expand

turn pages: next, previous.

The latter makes feasible the *browsing* of documents under user command. It helps in running menus, and makes feasible the able handling of embedded applications.

Window management makes feasible a distinction between *physical* and *logical windows.* A physical window displays one or more page(s) of a document. For instance, pressing the left switch of a mouse, the user brings to the screen a window menu. Moving the mouse, he points the cursor on the desired command which will be validated by pressing the middle key. This is a function similar to that of the Return key on the keyboard. Choosing the computing menu (as in Figure 5.2), the user reaches a second menu page. Once again, through one of the three keys on the mouse, the user commands the screen. Usually associated with the offer is a routine which permits adapting the device to the existing user programs.

Embedded Functionality

With the correct WS implementation, the user can interact with his WS through easy media: touch screen, graphic tablet, mouse, and eventually voice. He can select commands and feed-in data. WS software lets the user do graphing, word processing, calculating, list creation, and project scheduling, all on the same station. In a way totally transparent to the end-user, jobs can be brought to the top of a pile or placed underneath for future reference. Data can easily be exchanged among jobs.

Housekeeping chores can be effectively represented to the end-user by small pictures on the screen. Data, for example, can be thrown away when moved into the *wastebasket*, or can be saved on a *clipboard*.

Figure 5.3 sums up the functionality to be embedded in screen management, including the ability to handle windows. *Windows* are independent format handling devices which respond to standard input/output calls. They also answer commands to manipulate attributes such as location, size, font-usage, exposure, and keyboard status. Typically, a window is associated with the raster-scan device upon which it is displayed. Windows may or may not have a one-to-one relationship with processes.

Every window has an independent multifont map. The map attaches itself to a process group to which a signal is sent whenever: the window changes size or location, becomes exposed or covered, gains or loses current keyboard window status. Only the user has control over the windows in the system; but a window can be manipulated by a process in its process group or by a process with write permission on the window.

Upon creation, all windows are entered in the file system as character-special devices. In the directory they have a filename specified by their user-supplied label.

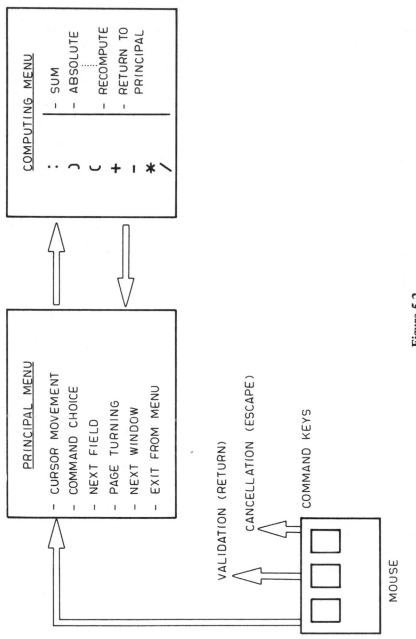

Figure 5.2

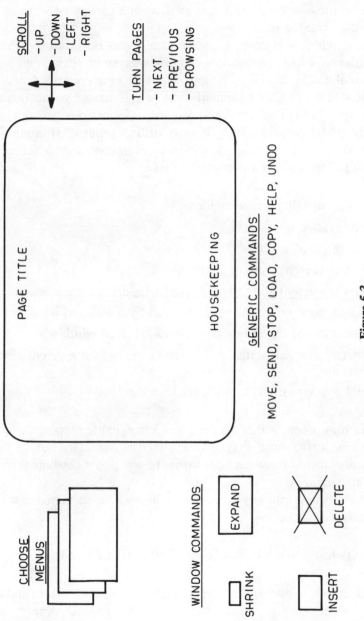

Figure 5.3

Windows are dynamic in that their location, size, exposure and font-map can be modified at any time under user/program control. When a window is created, it can be used in a variety of ways by the process that created it.

When a window is covered, output to it can be saved in a buffer and displayed when the window becomes exposed again. This way a process will not be halted by being output to a covered window.

Windows lead to the implementation of a simulated virtual memory environment allowing combinations of applications to run concurrently which would never fit into ordinary personal computers. User creation and control of windows is accomplished through a set of calls. These allow a user-process to

make and initialize a new window,

draw or erase a window,

insert a selected window,

obtain the current state of a window,

nodify the current state of a selected window,

select and manipulate the fonts utilized by a selected window,

read the state of the mouse device in a selected window,

obtain the current state of the display to which a given window belongs, and

switch keyboard input to a selected window.

Windows may occupy independent and changeable rectangles on the videoscreen surface and may overlap each other. Their usage helps users easily move between spreadsheet, word processing, graphics and other packages.

Through functional keys, the user will be able to manage generic commands:

MOVE, SEND, STOP, LOAD, COPY, HELP, UNDO, ...

The WS must support the appropriate vocabulary and make it feasible for the user to control the coherence of more complex commands. For its own management, the WS should gather statistics.

Depending on user requirements, WS must have logical capabilities for a number of functions to be done at a local level. Local functionality allows microfile editing, and this opens a totally different perspective than that traditionally supported by non-intelligent terminals.

Applications should be designed to eventually accommodate more powerful graphic modifier instructions to permit the rotation, scaling and transposition of portions of the displayed image. Instructions for generating images will be necessary not only for engineering but also for management applications. End-users will increasingly be able to generate and manipulate their own images using interactive devices.

It must be possible to search documents according to *search parameters* (filters); create, as mentioned, embedded functions specific to a given job; and provide WS with a multiple communications capability. Embedded applications must:

1. Reflect the fact that WS are designed for managers and professionals.

2. Account for the specific characteristics of the job to which they are dedicated.

3. Have a heavy graphics orientation, be menu-driven and use an easy way to cursor manipulation.

4. Simplify the handling of the screen; display commands; open or close a file; move a word or other information element.

5. Make it possible to create and maintain any type list in a personal database—the WS *microfile.*

6. Be supported by integrated software so that the user can cut what has been created by the use of one package, making it available to another.

7. Provide communications capabilities among WS through LAN and long haul networks; to reach text and data warehouses by means of gateways, as well as other company computers.

The range of embedded applications can be impressive. For instance, using a PC with graphic tablet data entry, the navigation company at Lago di Como has replaced the typical ticket issue through an interactive system.

Being informed of origin/destination, it automatically calculates the cost and issues the ticket. Another transport company provides its personnel with immediate updates on the location of transit shipments and/or vehicles.

With minimal training, a clerk can learn to access the local database on routes, delays, and transshipments, and also input updating information. Major customers can access authorized information directly without having to talk with someone in the trucking firm—thus determining the status of their shipments—or verify critical pickup/delivery schedules.

Workstations in finance and banking provide each loan officer with accurate, timely information on a customer's loan and account status. The officer updates his microfiles as transactions occur.

What is more, workstations can reach the smallest branch offices, operating online/standalone. They do away with the need for expensive private lines by running on switched networks, incorporating a simple modem dictated by the application.

New opportunities are made feasible through intelligent WS. Figure 5.4 gives an example. A furniture merchant has installed in his showroom a PC with a graphic tablet. The embedded application

accepts room layout references,

permits furniture selection with dimensional statistics in microfile,

makes feasible accept/reject decisions based on dimensions and layout, and

after acceptance, provides the possibility for optimization.

Embedded applications will be a basic requirement for executives who increasingly rely on portable computers that fit inside a briefcase, or full-scale micros that can be rented at hotels catering to business travelers.

Don'ts and Dos in WS Design

The study and implementation of a WS should be specific to the application it aims to assist, answering its requirements in an able manner. Yet, some general principles exist to guide the hand of the designer. In this section, we will consider the most important.

Let's first start with the *Don'ts*:

1. *Don't be superficial in projecting the new system.*

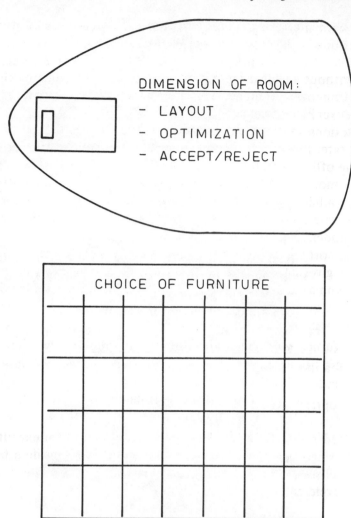

Figure 5.4 A furniture application on WS.

When changing over to more sophisticated systems, do the work methodically, not casually. Don't try to install a whole new line of hardware, a new operating system, and a new set of applications all at once. Undertaking too many changes in one shot is even more unadvisable when personnel is insufficiently trained.

It is particularly important to isolate the variables so that not too many of them change at the same time. This underlines the second issue:

2. *Don't bring up software/hardware too quickly.* Set up a pilot program followed by parallel testing.

Both prior to installation and during the transition it is vitally important to provide training. This helps to increase acceptance and improve overall performance.

Just as important is handholding. For the first 60 days it is good to maintain a *trouble desk,* with experts who can assist users when necessary on an oncall basis.

3. *Don't scare the user away from the system.*

If possible, employ voice input; if not, graphic tablet, touch sensing screens, or functional keys. It is also wise to give the user some options. Citibank in London did so quite successfully, offering the users a choice between an electronic pen and cursor.

To make the WS functions easier to assimilate, computer-based training material can run on the WS itself. What's more, WS level training can be downloaded and used by an employee whenever desired. Computer-based training can apply all the way from clerical job changes to the use of new decision support packages by management. It can also be successfully combined with recently announced storage media, such as videodiscs, making feasible the combination of dataframes and moving pictures.

4. *Don't overload the workstation* in regards to WS software/hardware and embedded applications.

The best advice is to keep the WS simple and low cost. Don't put hardcopy at the WS level unless absolutely necessary. If you really need hardcopy, then make it an image of the 80-column softcopy.

When projecting the WS, think that text, data, and graphics will be stored and processed at the level appropriate for the people who access it most. Thus, departmental files should be stored at the department level, such as the database of a local area network. Managers, professionals, and clerks might access and process the files by using their workstations in a terminal emulation mode. However, files used only by one person should be stored at the microfile level so that analyses will only access local storage, give fast response, and avoid bottlenecks.

This leads us to a list of *Dos*:

1. *Do answer the problems inherent to the workplace—at the workplace.*

Such positive action may require specific software/hardware answers such as hard discs at the WS level, the storage of frequently required programs on hard discs, and the provision of a strong communications discipline for text/data swapping with nearby and remote resources. Individual workstations will be of limited usefulness unless connected to local networks, which in turn are connected to higher level long haul networks.

With *logical networks*, things get more interesting. An example of a logical network is group service. An employee might log on to one logical network and have a variety of services available:

abbreviated addressing,

private data,

simultaneous viewing of the same information, etc.

Nonmembers of the group would not have access to this information even if on the same physical network. This enhances text/data privacy by means of closed user groups.

Logical networking also makes feasible signing onto another logical group of which one is a member, involving different users and different services.

2. *Provide easy, secure access to microfiles, local/regional databases and text/data warehouses and assure datacomm capabilities transparent to the user.*

A manager's principal requirement for communications is with his staff, with access to microfiles for limited use. With the exception of statistical references, there is no significant access requirement to major databases.

Professional requirements are the largest and most economically important, but they are also the most complicated because of their diversity. This has inhibited the development of satisfactory solutions.

Whether for managerial or clerical implementation, *action files* should be kept by the user. Entries into such a file are typically due to receiving or distributing a document. Part of the filing may be an entry into the follow-up file with the system automatically supplying an action due date or the user keying an action due date. The user must also be able to create entries in the action file that are not associated with documents—meetings, dates, appointments, and so on. He also may cause an automatic display or printing of the file according to a key of his choice.

While managerial requirements have often to do with time handling, the clerical/secretarial requirement is primarily for word processing and document handling tasks. Data retrieval and communications with other personnel working at keyboards are necessary. (This type of WS is today the best understood by vendors.)

Nevertheless, whether for managerial or for clerical purposes, the WS must be designed to:

3. *Be user-friendly: simple, easy to input, easy to retrieve, explanatory, prompting. This means selecting very carefully the man-machine interfaces.*

The system must support the self-training of users through computer-assisted techniques. *Prompting* facilities must be available to permit predefinition of procedures required to perform defined jobs. Aids for helping—error diagnosis, tutorials—must also be an integral part of the system interface to the user. The WS should include calculator capabilities to allow definition by the user of items related to data handling. The most common functions are predefined. This capability should also be used with text.

The embedded applications concept is just as valuable in this connection as in any other. Many office activities do not fit any single pattern and, this leads to an analysis of functions to determine what people were doing and where savings might be made. For instance, it was found that private secretaries supporting a single professional estimated that they spent only 26% of their time typing. By contrast, secretaries who supported more than four professionals estimated that 45% of their time was devoted to typing.

Embedded applications at the secretarial level may, for instance, focus on automated correspondence. In this case, the system must allow for the easy creation of form letters, letters composed of standard paragraphs, and letters automatically generated when a specified event occurs. It may also require facilities to allow the user to define, maintain, and use various lists.

Whatever the task to be accomplished, it must be presented to the user in a simple, effective manner. He should also be allowed to fail now or then without bringing the system down.

4. *Provide for security, system statistics, and diagnostics.*

With any online system, a security scheme is required to protect it from access by unauthorized persons. Since the system will store sensitive information—personnel data, profit figures, and so on—additional protection is needed to control access to this information by authorized users.

Facilities are also necessary to collect data about system use so that costs can be determined and, most importantly, the modular structure can be expanded to avoid bottlenecks with shared resources. Though the WS is dedicated to one person, other resources—such as databases, local and long haul communications links—will serve many. This very fact is also in the background of the security requirements.

Finally, WS diagnostics should run in two modes: A *customer mode* and a *service mode*. The latter is managed by field engineers or by customers with inhouse maintenance programs.

Among the tests provided in the customer mode are those for Video (displaying full screen pattern, using the bit-map option and color monitor when available), for floppy/hard disc drives (with file system operations so that user data is preserved), for the printer port (looking into the internal loopback capability without disturbing the printer), for the floating point processor (providing a confidence check), and for the communications port (using the internal loopback capability to isolate problems). Other customer mode tests may include the keyboard (verifying that all keys work), bar patterns (allowing adjustment of color, intensity, and tint on color monitors and intensity and contrast on monochrome monitors), and the system test, showing the status of all the hardware components.

The service mode typically has available all tests in the customer mode, plus disc tests (allowing more extensive testing, along with the ability to bypass the file system to test the entire disc surface) and printer tests (focusing on support of an external loopback connector and the printer itself, as well as communications tests of rather extensive capabilities including loopbacks). While due to mainframe practices these tests may sound like the vendor's responsibility, in a finely distributed environment they are the user's.

Chapter 6

SYSTEM ANALYSIS
FOR WORKSTATIONS

Introduction

In the near future, logical solutions and computer-based intelligence will be integrated into one knowledge system. Any serious, fundamental effort done today on WS design and system integration should account for this basic fact.

This is another way of stating that there are two essential ingredients in computers and communications technology.

1. The first regards how to apply knowledge to achieve goals. This provides the capability for intelligent behavior: processing text and data to solve our problems. That is what algorithms and programs are all about.

2. The second has two components: the miniaturization of the physical system that have this ability for intelligent action, and the very high level languages for machine programming.

Through the now developing advanced programming approaches, computer technology offers the possibility of incorporating intelligent behavior into computing machinery. Yet, the employment of high productivity programming tools and the use of commodity software is not enough. The organizational work to be done as a prerequisite is the most important.

A basic principle of which management should take due notice is that *unless a firm uses the most modern technology it will lose the fight for survival.* A corollary to this principle is that it takes much more than software/hardware acquisition to ride the wave of advanced technology. Solutions based on throwing money at the problem will remain inadequate unless the prerequisites are fulfilled.

It is the organizational work done prior to WS introduction that makes the difference between success and failure. Such organizational work must focus on computers and communications, but it must first solve the numerous, often complex problems associated with procedures, office systems, and methodology. Such solutions must be generic and account for the fact that soon computer-based workstations will be as popular as the telephone is today.

Office Studies

The primary goal of a system analysis of offices is understanding the way they function. This presupposes defining user needs, evaluating present tools, projecting the new logical/physical media and their impact, reorganizing the work, and providing guidelines for the usage of these tools: in short, placing emphasis on planning.

The system analyst should meet with the managers, the professionals, the secretaries and the clerks; analyse needs and requirements; produce an initial procedural description; develop a functional draft; iterate the interview process; review the results with the users; and finalize his proposal. Chances are the needed services in an office environment will involve:

1. At the secretarial level
   document creation
   document updating
   copying
   information searching

2. At the managerial and secretarial levels
   storage/retrieval
   information transfer
   digital voice communication
   recordkeeping
   follow-up
   mail handling

3. For primarily managerial purposes
   video conference
   business graphics
   time scheduling

information analysis

computation

voice annotation

Workstation implementation should be projected around these mainlines. Exceptions should attract particular attention: communications not received; lost or misplaced documents; discovery of erroneous data; noncompliance with current procedures; defective or obsolete rules; processes behind schedule; reversal of earlier decisions.

The collection of valid statistics is the next most important reference: time spent per function and who performs it; number of objects in process at any one time; time and effort spent in the various procedure phases; time elapsed for completion of a procedure; frequency of repetition; number of objects processed per time unit; timing and functional constraints. The same is true about the frequency of exceptions, references to alternate processing, the number of people involved per major function, updating procedures, and the size of personal databases.

A taxonomy of office tasks distinguishes among communications (content, media), databasing and document storage, and word processing (computing, process definition, help aids). A process taxonomy developed by INRIA distinguishes among read, listen, observe; check, review; study, analyze; correct, revise, edit; create, write; complete, form; interpret, translate; summarize, condense; expand, elaborate; calculate; copy, duplicate; file, record, transcribe; search, retrieve; decide, select, choose; organize, arrange; and code, classify.

Using this generic range of references and a comprehensive definition of office tasks, the analyst should proceed with the body of his study. The following three areas highlight a procedural sequence:

1. Study of workplace by sector

1.1 Identify the sectors

1.2 Detail their components

1.3 Examine their conversion to DP/WP

1.4 Evaluate their integration

1.5 Provide for online, interactive approaches

1.6 Make a proposal on a sector-by-sector basis

2. Examine in detail the paperwork flow

2.1 Establish current conditions

2.2 Identify the forms used

2.3 Bring into perspective the conditions under step No. 1

2.4 Design a forms integration to permit the use of new technologies

2.5 Examine alternatives: graphics tablet, touch sensing screens, voice input/output

2.6 Evaluate impact on database (microfiles, local central files)

2.7 Use the data dictionary

2.8 Provide interfaces to existing structures

3. Integrate the sector-by-sector and paperwork solution into a coherent aggregate

3.1 Develop comprehensive image

3.2 Propose systems solution

3.3 Evaluate effects on productivity: managerial, secretarial, clerical

3.4 Demonstrate access to and use of database

3.5 Project implementation priorities

3.6 Plan personnel training

3.7 Assure life cycle maintenance and dependability

3.8 Calculate costs and demonstrate savings on one-year basis and for life cycle

The emphasis on the study of paperwork flow is not at all accidental. It is a fundamental approach which has the advantages of modularity at different levels of reference and parallelism in handling asynchronous activities. It also helps identify data flow and control information.

The wisdom of using formalisms cannot be repeated too often. They should be developed and observed for all areas of activity, particularly for

communications

document retrieval

text preparation

personal computing

decision support, and

the use of analytical tools at large.

Let's take some examples to see the type of studies the system analyst should be doing. Communications may involve text, data, graphics, image, and voice. They can be *interactive,* with both parties online at the same time (simultaneous handling), or *deferred,* through stored messages which can be forwarded in accordance with a pre-established algorithm. Electronic message exchange, voice messaging, and computer conferencing are examples. Electronic message systems can be electronic mail (Email) or videotex. (The latter adds routing frames, color, and graphics to a basically Email facility.)

Electronic message systems give users almost instant relief from telephone lag, slow interoffice mail, and memo overload. Since so much managerial and professional time is spent in communications, they pay off quickly. Furthermore, properly tooled service offerings and packages are readily available.

In evaluating an electronic message system, the analyst must—as a prerequisite—establish if it is only for distributing documents among all users or if it is designed for person-to-person communications. He must also specify the formalisms and bylaws. For instance, experience suggests never to move exact numbers, such as 18.7%, through Email. Numbers should be converted to text: "eighteen point seven percent."

Work Simplification

Questions concerning workstation operation must be answered. What is the object work? The work hours? Who operates it? To which organizational structure does it belong? How long is information retained online and offline?

Other questions pertain to availability. Office systems must be available from early in the morning to late in the evening. This timeframe would not only accommodate early and late workers but also make the system available for people in other time zones and users who may travel or work at home.

A vital area of operational concern is security and protection. The system study must examine authorization and authentication. It must also set parameters relative to storage and time of access; control the amount of information retained in the active online system; and identify documents rolled in/out of the active system from/to an archive.

The analyst would have to take the information protection a step further. Information required by law to be retained would have to be designated and protected accordingly; text/data necessary to reconstruct the business in case of disaster would also have to be distinguished and protected. To counterbalance the complexity inherent in these references, the system analyst must pay significant attention to *work simplification methods*. The primary goal of work simplification is to progress to the point where automation is feasible in terms of practical implementation. Simplification has the potential benefit of offloading parts of the executive job on the WS, but the lack of adequate system study can lead to oversimplification.

Care should be taken to ensure a proper balance. Such a task is the more challenging as adequate methods do not exist currently to evaluate performance effectiveness. Research in this area would be fruitful. Future methodologies need to incorporate approaches for failure modes, effects analysis, and fault-tolerant designs. Still, by using available tools, the system analyst can nicely establish real needs at the WS level; study what technology offers by way of solutions; elaborate a budget; and online the timeplan.

Enough experience is available to define the requirement (data entry, inquiry, update), the data load, the proposed facilities, and the data communications solutions. Within this perspective, the analyst must have the experience to judge whether human potential will be adequate and what is needed to upgrade it.

Other questions in his mind should be: Will top management support his effort? What's the cost/effectiveness? How fast will the cost of the new system be recovered? What's the next step? The next system? All this adds up to a long, hard look and suggests the following steps as a procedural methodology:

1. Problem-oriented formulation
2. Reduction of problem complexity
3. Modularization of the established procedure

4. Search for standardized module by problem section
5. Generation of linkages
6. Checking for accuracy
7. Provision of routines to allow proper handling.

Standards and formalisms can both simplify and solidify the analyst's job. *Standards permit portability, taking first the application, then its programs, from one machine to the other. They also call for a clear policy.* (Portability implies that *only commodity software* is used, avoiding small specialized groups and the risk that when the machine changes the software must be thrown away—or when the programmer goes the programs deteriorate.)

(The negation to standards are the so-called "turn key" solutions in which the computer manufacturer uses *his own* OS which no other vendor employs. The problem with such vendors is not just that they sell for high prices and the user simply does not know how much HW/SW they sell him because it is bundled. The problem with turn keys and esoteric OS is *the total lack of portability to other equipments*—over and above being a very expensive solution.)

At the analysis level, standards and formalisms define the way in which the study should be conducted. Take text preparation as an example. For the last 10 years or so, text handling has been done by word processors. The new emphasis, however, is on the integration of functions into a system and on its possible use by professionals and managers. The processes involved in text preparation range from the organization of the text in the author's mind to the presentation of the formatted pages to the reader. Between these activities, there is plenty of room for the integration of new technologies.

Associated to text handling is information retrieval. This comprises all facilities that give the user access to database and document archives. It includes, but is not limited to, all the traditional storage media that may be provided as part of an office system. These must be described by the system analyst with special attention to how data can be integrated into other facilities, such as electronic mail or document production. They must also be tested in terms of results to be obtained through an interactive query package.

Effective studies in this direction do, however, call for attention to be placed on the fundamentals. As such, they underline the following steps as parts of a system analysis on interactive workstations:

1. Knowledge of the procedural system

2. Knowledge of the HW/SW components on which the procedural system will run

3. Search for procedures to reduce the application's complexity and size through specialization of interactive supports

4. Detailed study of data flow characteristics: source, destination, storage, retrieval, channeling, purging

5. Evaluation of response time and measures to hold it steady

6. Establishment of interactive tutorial for user guidance within a policy of explicit support (documentation and training)

7. Provision of appropriate control mechanisms by logical/physical nodes, spring points and sink point.

This study will have greater chances for success if there is a strong desire by management to participate in the design, development and tests, including a commitment to cooperate by all department staff members.

Since communicating WS have many interdepartmental characteristics, there should also be a reasonable amount of communication among department managers and the professional staff. This is necessary to better evaluate the distribution functions of text, data, graphs, image and voice. Just as important is the ability to easily create document databases that would later be accessed for search and retrieval. In this particular connection the multicommunications aggregrate should play a vital role.

Procedural System Analysis

Workstation implementation requires a coherent and cautious strategy. The key to success lies in the preparatory work.

The functional capabilities to be implemented should have a wide range of transaction handling, word processing, and other business-oriented functions at their disposal. They should be integrated into a cost/effective network, provide communication protocols, assure message processing, and be endowed with systems software. They should permit transmissions both between satellite locations and the central office as well as among remote locations. The distributed processing configurations should be able to use the same applications and should be flexible enough to accommodate growth without a major reinvestment in application software and user retraining.

Quite importantly, the WS network should lend itself easily to the development of new value-added applications and to expansion. A study of these issues typically involves:

1. general procedure;
2. qualitative evaluation of data processing requirements (in terms of management reports to be produced, customer orders/ confirmations, and so on);
3. both qualitative and quantitative requirements for data communications; and
4. both qualitative and quantitative requirements for databasing.

These four parts constitute the foundations of the projected implementation of computers and communications for the realization of any project. The mission of the Procedural System Analysis (PSA)—to be done with the user—is two-fold:

Provide a contractual understanding between the user and the developer of software for the implementation to take place.

Assure the background necessary for able system choices, particularly in regard to the OS, database management system (DBMS), hardware and software to be developed, and end-user functions (EUF) to be assured.

This interdependence among prerequisites, job specifications, and technical requirements is demonstrated in Figure 6.1.

Past the level of OS, DBMS, HW, SW, and EUF choices, comes the writing of the more detailed system specifications. It is not possible to proceed with program design until the aforementioned decisions have been made. This same reference is just as valid about mapping the logical structure of the files into the physical means to be provided.

If we have a valid DBMS able to do much of the file management work automatically, we need not worry about the handling issue. By automating the databasing activities, the DBMS relieves the analyst from doing so; but greater ease also accentuates the need for file design

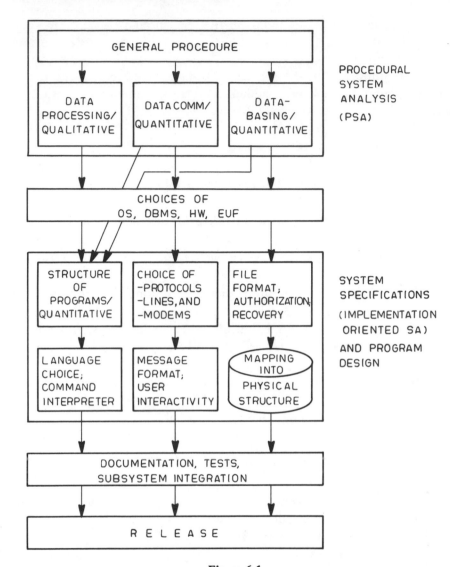

Figure 6.1

and specifications. Furthermore, interactive and communications-intense requirements place emphasis on a whole range of specifications: output formats, files, input formats, and messages. These have to be redesigned, integrated, and kept consistent. Message format, local networking, and user interactivity cannot be studied until the file format is decided. According to the advanced design principles in computers and communications: *a message is a file in the database and every file should be designed as a message.*

The result of using disperse documents prepared over time for typewriter handling can be disastrous. Such a practice—rather than helping the employee—may have increase the needed time for transaction. Any project which starts by retaining the "old forms" has to be returned to the drawing board until standard formats are developed, integrating different (often disperse) requirements into *one* properly planned form.

An example of how a careful study with specific goals can help simplify paperwork comes from an industrial firm. When seven years ago it was decided to put small minicomputers at the sales offices, the existence of 33 different forms handled by typewriters brought this project to a stop. As a result, it was necessary to carefully examine each document, looking in detail into the information elements which it contained, their functionality and destination. Following this, the 33 forms were reduced to three:

the first for accepting new clients;

the second as a unique sales order;

The third as a unique voucher.

Something similar is necessary for all projects, particularly so for those regarding complex operations. The aim should be to exploit to the fullest extent the computer power brought to the individual desk—together with access to databases (microfiles, local and central information elements) and with an efficient communication between workstations and among workstations and databases.

To the contrary, in terms of data processing, the study done at the PSA level provides no valid basis for calculating the steps which are necessary to do the programming work. The processing blocks must be projected first to establish a logical flow and to validate this flow. This must be executed prior to making estimates.

While the use of fourth generation languages relieves the need for a specification of the processing blocks, the detailed program design cannot be skipped. If nothing else, interactive and transactional characteristics of online systems impose prerequisites and imply choices. Two references are outstanding: *response time* calculations oblige an emulation of the online environment, and *user friendly* solutions underline the wisdom of keeping the end-user in the design picture. Furthermore, new technologies bring forward another prerequisite: The choice of the programming language to be used must be made prior to a factual and documented evaluation of the work which needs to be done.

The impact of the programming language is so great that *any evaluation of the needed work, in terms of skill and man-months, is impossible without knowing in which language it will be executed.* Quite evidently, the choice of the programming approach should center on a very high level language (VHLL).

Process Planning

Process planning specifications go well beyond the procedural analysis phase and involve both systems design issues and implementation perspectives. The two subjects are interrelated.

It may not be evident that the SW/HW components have much to do with the daily startup of the system, yet this is actually the case. The same is true of system backup on a scheduled basis.

A network of workstations does not operate on its own. Recovery tasks are required. Maintenance is a steady job. User education and liaison are important, and so is equipment coordination.

To whoever gains WS experience, the above operational requirements become evident very quickly. Therefore, it is wise to account for them. Process planning involves:

1. Establishment of process characteristics
2. Identification of the subprocesses
3. Specification of the subschemas
4. Definition of data validity requirements
5. Establishment of precedence among subprocesses
6. Elaborations on efficiency, uptime, and dependability.

A map like the one presented in Figure 6.2 is helpful in projecting the layout both of *routing frames* (menus) and of *infopages*. It also assists in projecting the system prompts and help pages.

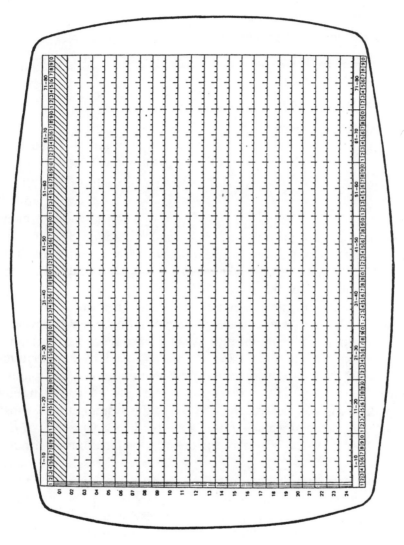

System Analysis for Workstations ■ 91

Figure 6.2

Output formats, file structures, and input formats bring into perspective the need for information element (IE) planning. This requires:

1. Identification of objects to be handled
2. Elaboration of object attributes
3. Definition of permissible range of values for the attributes
4. Establishment of relations between these objects
5. Definition of the subschemas
6. Integration of subschemas into a schema
7. Specification of the rules governing the relation of the sub-schemas among themselves, to the schema and to the process(es)
8. Elaboration of security and recovery procedures for all IE involved.

The whole area of records management and protection of corporate text/data assets must be accommodated. We have already spoken of the need for authorization/authentication. The prototype provides testing grounds also for this issue.

Using a prototype, executives and secretaries sign on. The system tests the WS rights, as well as the authorization of the sender/receiver to handle specific IE. Then, in response to a set of prompts, it presents an initial display as in Figure 6.3, to be followed by an extended display—after the choice made in the first menu page.

Since the system will request keywords and special handling instructions (confidential, receipt required) the system analyst must project them in the process planning activity. The same is true of the facilities necessary for WS users for creating memos online through the display.

A *memo entry* option prompts the user to enter descriptive information, memo content, and addressees' names. At the completion of this process, the WS automatically distributes the document to each recipient, whether individually named or on a distribution list. A descriptive entry is immediately posted in the *mail queues* of the recipient(s). This posting is the equivalent of almost immediate delivery of documents to the recipient's desk.

Besides distributing documents, the system automatically stores a permanent record of each message. This record is indexed for later

```
PAGE ID  XX.XX                        DATE  XX.XX.XX
                                      HOUR    XX.XX




                        INITIAL DISPLAY

           DEPRESS FUNCTION TO SELECT NEXT ACTION

               1.  FILE SEARCH (RETRIEVE)

               2.  REVIEW HOLD QUEUE (SUSPENSE FILE)

               3.  ENTER INFORMATION (MEMO)

               4.  FORWARD MEMO (EMAIL)

               5.  REVIEW INCOMING COMMUNICATIONS

               6.  REVIEW TIMEPLAN (SCHEDULE)

               7.  TERMINATE SESSION (SIGN OFF)
```

Figure 6.3

retrieval by the originator and recipients, and becomes a reliable substitute for the traditional hardcopy files.

The indexing of documents by the descriptive parameters keyed during entry provides the ability to retrieve documents by originator to produce the equivalent of an originator's chronological file, and by keywords for a *project* (cross reference) *file*. Documents received from external sources and containing text, data, graphics, and images can be indexed the same way, filed and retrieved by the same search methods.

In years past, these activities had to be programmed. Today, they are available in electronic mail, document handling, and word programming packages. Still some programming will have to be done. Programming language planning calls for:

1. Choice of a very high level (fourth generation) language

2. Definition of mapping procedures

3. Specification of required resources and their management

4. Elaboration of rules for formulating and representing information

5. Establishment of rules for man-information communication.

The basic technical issues involved in program design show why it is premature to talk of work estimates in terms of man-months of effort and calendar months to completion *prior* to having examined what is available in packages and library routines—and having made the choice of the programming language.

It is helpful if program design projections are organized in the following manner:

1. Processing proper (DP)

2. File handling (DB)

3. Datacomm (DC)

4. End-user functions (EUF)

5. Utilities for DP/DB/DC.

For planning purposes, a compiler instruction typically corresponds to seven or eight assembler instructions. A database language statement corresponds to some 80 assembler instructions, or 10:1 compared to, say, Cobol. This is not programmers' time but lines of code. Programmer productivity is much higher, usually increasing 15 to 60 times when using a database language as contrasted to Cobol, with a ratio of 30:1 to 40:1 that may be valid in most cases.

Such statistics can be helpful in calculating programming time in man-month *and* calendary months—*after* developing the program design prerequisites of which we have spoken. These statistics represent *ready programs*: fully tested and properly documented. Testing and documentation takes about 60% of the total time.

Prototyping

Twenty years ago, *simulation* was used as a working model, the abstraction and idealization of a physical system which we could study through computers prior to building the system itself. This followed a long tradition from the 1940s when (analog) simulation was done through differential analyzers, to the 1950s with scale models, and into the 1960s with digital simulation.

Prototyping is also a working model—but of a logical system. In fact, the prototype is the program's specification. It is a *dynamic specification*, not a static, rigid document (like the classical system analysis).

Since prototyping is computer-supported, it is faster to do prototyping than develop paper documents—and the prototype is in itself a partially completed system. It can be run on the machine the final program will be running, but it is not optimized.

Typically, prototyping is done through shells and DBMS frontends. The best tool to do prototyping is that software which manages our data and allows us to access our data in the most effective manner:

1. With the first, second, and third (HLL) generations of programming languages, the software was limited by hardware technology.

2. With the fourth generation languages (4GL, VHLL) the software exploits hardware technology, particularly the large, versatile memory capacity of the computer.

This characteristic will be further strengthened through fifth generation languages (5GL) based on *expert systems*—which start becoming popular in 1985, but will need another five years to market maturity.*

Through the *human window* which characterizes expert system implementation we are very close to human factors breakthroughs. This will call for a significant amount of prototyping, which is another way of saying how important this concept is.

From processing proper to human interfaces, there are considerable advantages in proceeding with *prototype design*. A good prototype is:

small enought to implement,

large enough to impress,

cheap enough to get funded, and

urgent enough to get commitment.

Let me recapitulate the prototype reference. In contrast to classical DP, prototypes supply a solution to part of the problem, but they can

---

*Yet, it is most advisable to start right now developing and employing expert systems. It will take a good five years to master the art.

be delivered early in the process of development. Experience teaches that it is very useful, at that stage, to have a view of the application.

If we wish to put black-on-white which will be the most likely main drives in the 1986–1990 timeframe, we can write:

1. *The use of prototypes*, as implemented in engineering.
2. *Computer communications*, increasingly characterized in ways practiced by humans.
3. *System integration* of communications media, databases, processing routines, end user functions.

Interactive WS are key components in everyone of these references. That is why it is so important to learn them well and use them in a rational manner.

The so-called *dark tube* surveys many companies started conducting by mid 1985 to find out how many of the PC they bought are used and when, are ill-directed. They look at the symptoms rather than at the origins. The origin of "dark-tubeness" is *computer illiteracy—that much among end-users as among computer professionals*. As a medicine, prototyping can be of help.

Chapter 7

HUMAN ENGINEERING

Introduction

The semantics of a good end-user interface must be consistent with the semantics of the work being done. The syntax of the interface should be as natural as possible, appearing intuitively obvious to the user.

The syntax must be uniform and consistent within the context of the WS. Accomplishing the same function by multiple variant forms must be minimized, and the use of variant forms for similar functions eliminated.

The system must allow selectable levels of aid and guidance for users of different degrees of expertise. Friendly software is particularly important during the learning period, but experts should not be burdened with conventions for aiding people in training. A user operating in the tutorial mode, for example, may require many more transmissions between his terminal and a processor than the experienced executive.

In addition, the end-user language needs to be easy to comprehend, use, and remember. Organizations that offer end-user languages point out how quickly employees can learn to use them, usually within a few days. This ease of learning is important because end-users may refuse to employ systems that require them to remember complex commands or procedures. At the same time, each user entry should perform lots of work. Such an entry can be a single key, a short command, a menu selection or the touch of a finger to a video screen.

Soon after learning to use the basics, end-users will want to perform more complex operations. The more powerful their entries are, the more they will use the system, and the more they will obtain from it.

Ergonomic Factors

As the user community expands beyond DP specialists to include managers, professionals, secretaries and clerks with little technical training, human factors play a large role. The first evidence of attention to *human engineering* dates back to World War II, and can be found both in the United States and in England. The design of pilot cockpits and their instrumentation is one example; anthropometrics is another.

Until serious experiments took place, there was little scientific evidence to prove what designers only knew intuitively: That environmental design affects behavior. Hence, the design of the office and most specifically of the workplace can be an effective tool.

Human engineering can improve productivity and the quality of work life. It helps quantify the impact of office equipment as it affects an organization's bottom line. Human engineering is also instrumental in isolating those aspects of the environment that matter, understanding how and why they do so.

The search for valid solutions in the design and management of the office environment helps reveal issues affecting overall job satisfaction—either directly or through job performance. Experimental studies usually employ control groups to increase the validity of findings. They focus on

Architecture and general layout

Interior and environmental design

Psychology: social, industrial, environmental

Statistics on organizational development and administrative issues

Equipment design as applied at the workplace.

Behaviorally, supportive design can now be studied on the basis of logic and research. The goal must be to establish the office as a working tool and, beyond that, as an investment which has a return. This means we must focus our attention on those design factors known to affect job satisfaction and job performance. Preferences for colors and materials must be observed, such as leaning toward pastels and natural materials like wood and fabric. Lighting also affects environmental satisfaction and all vision related aspects of job performance. Clerical workers with the most demanding visual tasks are the least satisfied with lighting. The overall visual quality or image and a sense of orderliness and cleanliness are the elements that matter most.

Rotating and tilting screens for adjustment are recommended. Screens should be selected for grain factor, color, light emitting efficiency and persistence.

It is wise to watch the warm air flowing from fans. The use of document holders is advisable, inclined between 15° and 17° to the horizontal according to the operator's visual acuity.

Glare effects must be controlled. They result from a high range of luminances in the visual field and too many windows. We can reduce glare with etched glass, filters, and optical coatings.

Slim keyboards are better for elbow/wrist positioning. The tactile feed should be preferred for keystrokes, and a detachable keyboard gives more flexibility to adapt to one's working habits.

Ergonomic measurements have focused on pointing devices: joystick, mouse, keyboard and function keys. Figure 7.1 is based on test results obtained in French experiments, and compares the effects of three different devices in terms of positioning time and target distance.

Positioning time is one design factor. Low error rates, easy-to-remember functions, lucid displays, and fail-safe commands are other crucial issues.

Sign-on procedures must be quick and simple. As already stated, response times on terminals must be low (generally, less than five seconds). Users should feel confident of not being able to damage the system with a minor mistake. Any potentially serious error must be caught by the system.

Many organizational issues must be considered. Interactive, computer-based systems are reducing the need for simultaneity in organizations. People no longer have to be physically present at the same time and place to do their jobs.

Examples of system flexibility are the *editing functions* being supported: cursor up, down, right, left; clear screen; erase to end of field; character insert mode on/off; delete character in field/line; new line; forward/backward field tab; home function. (The latter is intended to move to the most important field on the screen.)

An indent function is helpful to move the cursor one tab stop to the right of its current position, setting the *newline* left margin to the current column. This is important in tabulation and in word processing.

Other helpful features include attribute bytes for numeric input fields (unformatted screens have no attribute bytes). Attribute

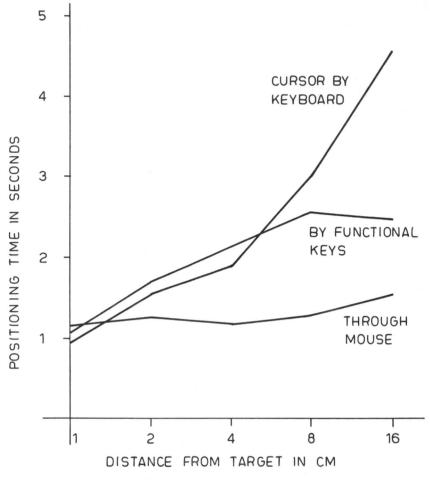

Figure 7.1 Cursor control.

highlighting can be extended into a significant range of functions. Skill/nonskip, swap of field tab, suppress pacing, bell function, and controllable indicators are but a few examples.

Guidance in Interactive Design

The user-perceived quality of interactive systems can be defined by describing essential user requirements. Each dimension is defined by a set of system properties, each taking values indicating its relevance for the quality of the system and the services it offers.

Research projects have brought in evidence the usefulness of the following criteria for the evaluation of an interactive system:

1. Supply *help features* pertinent to any dialogue situation.
2. When requested, provide *explanations* in different detail and format.
3. Explain each command and subcommand upon user request.
4. Give clearly arranged presentation of systems functions.
5. Provide global information about the *functional range* of the system.
6. Assure enough *user guidance* for the dialogue.
7. Supply information about the current system status, if desired.
8. Admit interruptions of a task to start or resume another task (priority, pre-emptying).
9. Admit cancelling of process without detrimental side effects.
10. Allow abortion of particular dialogue steps or processes.
11. Have a syntactically homogeneous command language.
12. Have a command language easy to remember.
13. Make repetitive or routine input unnecessary.
14. Have a data management system that obviates as far as possible the need for the user to perform clerical and housekeeping activities.
15. Manage formatting, addressing, and memory organization without bothering the user.
16. Accept free-formatted command input.
17. Be tolerant towards erroneous user input.
18. Have a command language easy to understand and easy to apply.
19. Provide flexibility in task handling.
20. Allow the user to extend the command language.
21. Allow the user selective access to the task stack.
22. Provide reduced input/output according to user's training level.
23. Allow the user to define his set of system functions.

24. Provide shorter ways for trained user to perform his tasks.

25. Permit user to define some particular end-use status.

26. Allow the user to make background processes visible.

27. Permit clustering of commands with a new name.

28. Assure fault tolerance.

29. Insist only on partial retyping if previous input was erroneous.

30. Give error messages with correction hints.

31. Enable the user to submit concatenated commands as input.

32. Accept reduced input when actions are to be repeated.

33. Give error messages in full text.

34. Give decision aids if tasks cannot be executed as desired.

35. Enrich the displayed information by means of encoded messages.

Safeguards must be assured to enhance the user's ability to do productive work. Results must be enhanced with the least inconvenience to the user, as the aggregate user time is more costly than the computer time.

A basic consideration in projecting interactive systems is that not only some of the authorized users will work with the system at the same moment, but also a small fraction of them will account for the largest share of available resources.

Statistics taken with interactive systems indicate that less than 10% of the users consume about 75% of the computing resources. Such curves characterize the distribution of computing usage in many installations, and should be kept in mind in system design. Users should always be brought into the picture. For instance, to overcome fear of the system, an American company let each manager learn how to run a simple conversational program. They all became excited at the system's possibilities, whereas they did not understand the printouts they were getting in the past.

Focusing on the top 10% of computer users, we find that a small fraction of their interactions dominates their demand for CPU-intensive operations. Systems design should account for this fact.

The bulk of the interactions involve I/O and query-type communications. The following considerations pertain to the design of an interactive system in terms of user requirement, programming necessities, and operations.

1. As far as the user is concerned, the instructions on terminal manipulation must be simple and easy for persons not trained in programming.

2. All housekeeping functions must be performed automatically and be clear to the user.

3. Automatic fault recognition and malfunction correction must be provided; neither should cause lengthy interruptions.

4. The system must be supported by a file handler providing access to data files without causing delays in interactive activities.

5. I/O that do not follow prescribed data forms (formats) must be reported to the user with clear diagnostic messages.

6. All software concerning inquiry/response functions must be clear to the user.

7. The same is true of the ability to update data files and to create new files, so that data collection activities can take place under system control.

8. To minimize implementation time and cost, any generalizations not imperative to the utility of the system should be dropped.

9. Maintenance requirements should be minimized by structuring the system so that changes are easy to make, and in a layered fashion.

10. The interface between the user and the interactive system must be simple, and must provide the user with a clear understanding of his duties relative to the system.

11. Because of the high volume of work to be performed on an online facility, requirements must be kept small in terms of memory utilization.

12. Good recovery procedures must be provided so that if the system stops, the fault is corrected, and the service returned to the user within a matter of minutes.

13. A file save and restore procedure must assure that current and valid data exists in the system data files at all times.

14. "Handshaking" functions must be included, i.e., ready to send/receive, ACK, fault recognition and retransmission, and a polling subroutine which controls activity between the computer and the terminal(s).

15. A buffer control routine is necessary to act as a traffic officer, maintaining queues of both incoming and outgoing messages.

16. A translation routine, e.g. converting ASCII to BCD or vice versa, must be available.

17. A logging routine is necessary. The log is used for accounting, statistical and recovery purposes.

18. An interface with the accounting system must be provided for an equitable way of charging the user.

19. The interface with other, existing products should be studied and worked-out before query-type implementation.

20. The use of intelligent terminals and of standard procedures is a recommended practice.

The criteria of success of any interactive system is to relate almost 100% to the end-user facility. One design factor is whether or not nontechnically trained managers make effective and regular use of the system. Another is the amount of time managers spend working online on their problems.

Graphics and Color

Once an area more or less reserved to larger companies with impressive computer budgets, interactive solutions (whether text, data or graphics) are now accessible to everyone. The user has his choice of terminals and a variety of packaged software systems.

Once mainly used as a design aid for engineering departments, graphics has become an important means of communicating to any level of management, regardless of the organization's size or type of activity—and the executive's own computer experience.

Graphics at the managerial WS level should be menu-driven. It should be possible to use them self-standing or in connection with other routines, making possible a multitude of graphic designs. Graphics software should:

Draw diagrams according to direct input or from file references calculated from other programs.

Change, complete, or rearrange files through a built-in data editor.

Automatically calculate diagram details.

Secure, edit, and print diagram definitions.

Enrich the diagrams with headlines and explanatory text.

The manager, rather than scanning voluminous printed reports, can use computer-based interactive color terminals summarizing financial conditions, revealing marketing trends and generally managing information effectively and quickly.

Graphic presentation helps to reduce data. Graphs on a single visual display can effectively represent many pages of tabular information. Formatting methods can increase comprehension by emphasizing the quality rather than the quantity of information.

Decision support environments are enhanced through graphic capabilities; long tables are often difficult and tedious to read and follow, and are ineffective in revealing strong and weak points. Graphics can tremendously aid in gaining management's attention and understanding by clarifying trends and magnitudes. Exception reporting aids the reader's retention, consolidates data from multiple sources, and focuses attention on significant events.

Interactive solutions make it possible to redraw trend curves and chart management indicators with new or revised data without having to start from scratch. What's more, the end-user can sit at a terminal and design, modify or produce graphics quickly and easily. He can display newly entered data, integrate information automatically extracted from diverse files, take a quick look at historical trends, modify assumptions by doing visual "what ifs," and glance into the future. All this can be done online in a user-friendly manner if three key problems are addressed by the designer:

1. Data presentation
2. "What *if*" experimentation
3. Graphical solutions.

In the past, graphics have been reserved for special occasions simply because of the high cost of and delays associated with preparing them manually. Every time a new chart was needed, an artist had to do it. But computers can do graphics and color presentations at high speed and with great effectiveness.

With computer-based tools, most business systems start with eight colors which is adequate for basic applications, though the greatest color flexibility comes from the *palette* approach: the user can select the displayable colors from a larger number, usually 64.

With a given application, such as budgeting, tracking information or comparative data can even be assigned a specific color. This results in more impact and greater comprehension.

Resolution can include such factors as the number of pixels on the screen, total refresh memory size, viewable memory size, and the addressing range of the input commands, though it typically describes the number of pixels on the screen. Resolution has a direct bearing on picture quality and the amount of information that can be displayed.

Of the low, medium and high resolutions available, a medium-resolution display of, say 512x256 (rows down by the number of pixels across), should be a starting place for all but the simplest graphics needs. Higher resolution ranges are 640x480, 640x512, and 1,280x1024 pixels.

Colorgraphic presentations can be inexpensively distributed to a large number of people by using an output device that prints on plain paper. Depending on whether the color graphic data is used as it appears on the screen or is distributed as hardcopy, there are a variety of choices.

A common device for entering data into the graphics system is the keyboard. When the information we want to enter already exists in pictorial form, we can enter it directly with the aid of a graphic tablet. Other types of cursor controllers—trackballs, light-pens and joysticks—make it easier to enter and manipulate data on the screen.

Important features for control systems are:

entity detection,

display list processing,

viewing transformation,

decluttering,

clipping, and

pan and zoom.

Entity detection permits the user to identify objects on the screen by simply steering a cursor to them. The computer is then interrupted and given the cursor coordinates, from which it invokes the entity detect mode and display lists that draw the objects to be sensed.

Display list processing permits downlining load pictures or sub-pictures and then calling them to the screen with a single instruction or keyboard function. This way, a user-defined menu might be displayed when an assigned key is struck.

Viewing transformation lets the user define his picture in terms of a world coordinate system. The WS projects that picture onto the screen in terms of a fixed virtual coordinate system that is potentially much larger than the refresh memory or screen resolution.

Decluttering keeps the picture clear by automatically adding or subtracting detail as the scale is changed. In more expensive graphic systems, lines can be automatically filtered out, for instance, when the picture is scaled up or down.

Clipping constrains the picture to an arbitrary rectangle. Due to local viewing transformation capabilities on the display, this is essential because the viewport (graphics area) may be exceeded as the picture is enlarged. A clip window may be set by the user to provide a split-screen capability. This way, annotation or menus can be drawn on one part of the screen while displaying graphics on another.

Pan and zoom are real-time interactive video functions. Graphics WS provide useful zoom ratios.

Existing graphics tools are useful for a more effective management of operations, and management should avail itself of this opportunity. These tools include break-even charts, quality control charts, time series, histograms and pie charts, the plot of statistical tests, Gantt charts, PERT/CPM, line balancing, stock control (limits and re-plenishment), financial analyses, critical ratios, and trend lines.

To be effective, graphics presentation tools require software support and user awareness. To do the editing and graphics prepa-ration, we must create the proper space on the computer, instruct the user on how to manage the space given to him, provide the native commands needed to do this operation, and assure a trans-mission time for the creation of the basic images.

Working together, the user and the system analyst will need to lay down the preparatory work for graphic information. There are problems of presentation, update, of access techniques (that's what the graphics software should make simple for users) and of *privacy/security* to guarantee data protection.

Let's take a management environment as an example. Assume that data and graphics will be available to the end-user through a simple, easy-to-follow data and image protocol. The following issues come into perspective:

1. Data entry requirements and relative choices (mouse vs. light-pens vs. keyboard, etc.).
2. Database organization for graphics.
3. Types of presentation forms to be chosen, including color.
4. Graphics presentation software (or firmware) able to handle a variety of presentation schemes through programmed functions.
5. An online editor for exception processing.
6. Bulk update where downloading from a mainframe is the best procedure.

This is only a partial list of requirements. We should keep in mind that this is a mobile business and, as such, it needs workshops, the availability of a design database, editing and updating approaches, and graphics training.

Chapter 8

OPERATING SYSTEMS FOR PCs

Introduction

The first generation of personal computers was characterized by 8-bit microprocessors. But the 8-BPW capability is now irrelevant for nearly all users. Also, several companies making 8-BPW add-on boards for PCs have had little impact or sales.

The second generation of PCs were 16 BPW/8-bit buses (Intel 8088) and 32 BPW/16-bit buses (Motorola 6800) hybrids.

Since then, the market has moved so fast that a *third* generation of PCs will be out the next couple of years. These will use more sophisticated versions of the new concept of OS designed for their predecessors. This is a major departure from past practices where the same operating system was used on mainframes and minis, "squeezing" the OS of the former on to the latter. The result of this squeeze was a complex operating system, so the question arose of how to provide competent computer operators for the minicomputer sites. However, the object should have been operatorless minicomputers to avoid the cost and staffing problems of professional operators at the remote sites.

The new generation of OS specifically designed for PCs avoid these pitfalls. They also make feasible, within a LAN concept, the implementation of a range of different DP engines operating on different OS and/or different varieties of the same software.

Operating systems function as intelligent interpreters between end-users and machines. As Figure 8.1 demonstrates, on the OS will rest a wide range of vital services. Under this perspective, we will examine the basic aspects of what is currently commercially available in the PC field.

Tough Competition and New Releases

Most application programs (AP) are thought to run under an OS. In reality, they run over the OS which actually mediates between the

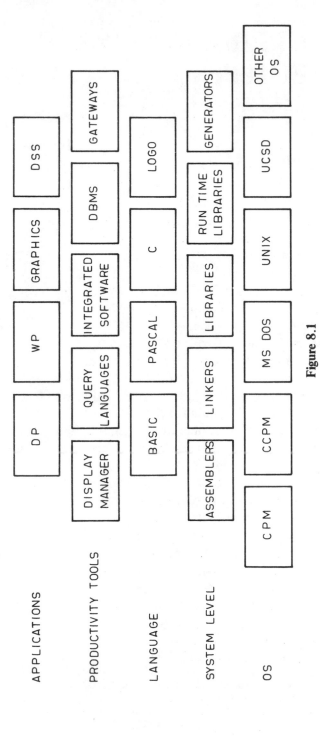

Figure 8.1

AP and the machine. This is equally valid whether we talk of mainframes, minis or micros. There is, however, a difference. While for mainframes and micros the vendor is responsible for providing the OS, in the PC class the OS is offered by independent software companies (sometimes promoted by the hardware manufacturer).

Competition among the PC makers is even more fierce than that among minicomputer manufacturers, resulting in frequent and substantial increases in price/performance. The same is true of the OS vendor for microcomputers.

PC competition is fostered by the widespread adoption of standard portable operating systems that have features well-matched to the capabilities of more powerful microcomputers. On the other hand, the orientation by OS vendors toward one or another type of microprocessor—and the PC using it as *their* engine—enhances the competition among PC manufacturers. End-users (particularly third-party organizations), original equipment manufacturers (OEM), and systems houses whose assets are the software packages they develop are keenly aware of this fact. When they build products to run under one of the portable OS, their key motivation is the freedom to move from one machine to another.

The best microprocessors available today are the Intel 8086 and 80X86 and the Motorola 68000, with the Zilog Z8000 a distant third. The custom-made LSI, locking the user into a one-vendor product line, are quite unpopular.

The most common commercially available operating systems are: MS DOS, Unix, CPM, and with UCSD a distant fourth.

Here again, the different custom-made OS are fully unwanted. No wonder that when systems houses set out to develop applications for PCs, they use one of the portable operation systems.

A new culture of applications software and of programmer experience surrounds these packages. Their developers try to satisfy advanced customer requirements, and the increasingly sophisticated offerings of MS DOS, CPM, Unix and their clones seem to be the best way for gaining acceptance and to harness the power of the high-end PC. The state of development of these programs is constantly in flux, as is the art of programming languages for the implementation of applications software.

Some years ago with the 8-BPW engines, Basic was mastering about 70% of all applications. This is no more the case. Even at its point of origin—the schools and colleges where it was taught to students—Basic is now challenged by LOGO, a LISP language. LOGO and C also appeal to the sophisticated user—with DP/WP integration in mind—and to the system houses writing horizontal software. The bulk of vertical development is held by Pascal.

MS DOS and CPM

We said that, like any computer, the PC must be supervised and controlled by an OS. We also underlined that with microcomputers the operating system is not inherent to the computer's hardware. It is a competitive commercial offering able to manage all facets of the computer's use. The OS typically controls the creation, removal, and progress of tasks, and the exceptional conditions arising during the operation of a task. Arithmetic or machine errors and interrupts are examples.

The OS typically allocates hardware resources and provides access to software: file editors, compilers, DBMS (if any), utilities, and communications routines. These software resources comprise the computer's personality from the user's viewpoint. The OS also provides protection, access control and security of stored information.

While these tasks are not new, there is a great difference between a born OS supplied by the computer manufacturer and a commercial option. In the former case, operating systems are usually unique to a specific computer brand. In the latter, different brands use the same OS.

Here is the challenge. The type of machine, the name of the vendor, *and* the microprocessor being used make a big difference. Not all systems run under all types of equipment. This, in turn, influences the choices to be found in terms of packages—as well as the performance of the machine.

In the 8-BPW machines, the fragmented CPM 80 market had so many different models that software developers often spent more time writing installation variations than on the main program. To the contrary, 16-BPW hardware has moved strongly toward not only a single operating system—Microsoft's MS DOS—but also a single machine design, IBM's PC.

The potential applications base is much greater under MS DOS than CPM 86. The de facto standard today is that of a single user and a single task. The CCPM gives up to four tasks.

In choosing an OS, if possible take Unix or Xenix with a user-friendly shell; alternatively, choose MS DOS. (CPM is more of a program development environment.) Also to be counted is the strategy of applications software firms. Make the software package first for the IBM PC (which means MS DOS) then for other PC brands.

There is another way of looking at the same subject. To a major extent, the CPM success story in the 8-BPW computers was program portability between PCs based on the 8080 and Z80. This opened up a new perspective of *sideways compatibility* among engines with heterogenous processors, but this time is now past.

Many problems of CPM Release 2.2 have stemmed from the scant version that Digital Research provided to ensure portability. It is left to the individual hardware manufacturer to come up with operating systems enhancements, including user-friendly interfaces.

Vector Graphic has been the first PC manufacturer to offer an improved CPM initiating the use of dual 64K memory boards for Z80 machines. The second 64K of memory on a Vector Graphic hold the operating system, I/O buffer areas, and operating utilities, leaving room for larger programs and models on the first, main memory board. The second board also acts as cache memory.

Recently, however, Digital Research developed CPM 3.0. This release has user-friendly features, including time and data stamps on files, a help facility, prompts for each part of a system command, and file searches that automatically extend over all disc drives. CPM 2.2 lacks error recovery facilities, whereas CPM 3.0 provides not only automatic diskette log-in but also extended error recovery. CPM 3.0 also has other improvements, such as multisector disc reads and writes and larger maximum file sizes. These let the computer use a hard disc to its full potential instead of just as an extra-large floppy, as is the case with UCSD.

While CPM remains the king of the 8-BPW engines, it has so far failed to master the 16-BPW OS market. At the same time, MS DOS and its subsequent releases are expected to defeat CPM 86. Today, far more applications software runs on MS DOS, and it is not likely that CPM 86 will be able to catch up.

Yet, some features of CPM 86 have been superior. For instance, it incorporates a graphics kernel that takes standardized descriptions of graphics from the software and draws the corresponding image on the screen with the capabilities of the hardware at hand.The applications programmer need no longer adapt graphics routines to each different micro. Eventually, this feature will undoubtedly see wide use and find its way into all major operating systems.

Personal computers using Motorola 68000 chips are more powerful than the 8088 and 8086/8 micros—but sales and software support have been slow. Apple and Radio Shack, by supporting 68000-based micros, left holes in their product lines, missing large areas of the main market.

With the software-intense third generation PCs waiting in the wings, hardware should begin losing importance over the next couple of years. By then, what a micro can do with working software will be more important than its microprocessor.

The Battle of the OS

The fast-developing environment which we are discussing will be the battleground of software products and of operating systems and horizontal and vertical routines.

If developments remain limited in scope, probably no single OS will totally overpower the rest, just as no high level language has eclipsed the rest of the field. In this case, the typical microcomputer will have an OS in firmware, whether it be MS DOS, CPM, Unix, UCSD Pascal, or some other. All signs point toward tough competition and, with it, fast development in functionality. This will simply become an economic necessity because the ultimate driving force in this market is software, not hardware.

Keep in mind that hardware is the means to the software end. Good software ultimately creates a hardware base to take advantage of it. The reverse is not necessarily the case.

MS DOS, Unix, and CPM will be the dominant operating systems mainly for 16-BPW engines. Though 8-BPW machines will not disappear for some years (there are economic arguments for their longevity), the 16-BPW and 32-BPW engines will overtake them. The battle of the OS will be fought for this type of equipment.

One of the new features to be supported is *concurrent processing*. In 1983, CPM 86 first incorporated concurrency capabilities. Concurrent CPM (CCPM) is an enhancement of CPM 86; it can run four programs simultaneously.

Such a multitasking idea is powerful, but it has made little progress. Users find that rapid switching from one program to another emphasizes inconsistencies in the interface; that is, the way programs use screens, keyboards, commands, and syntax. For example, the same key might save a file to disc in one program but erase a line in another.

Concurrent CPM has been designed with a *single user* environment in mind. In contrast, MPM (by the same software manufacturer) addresses itself to multiuser applications. (The comments I got on this issue is that MPM is a very poor system.)

CCPM's advantage rests in its ability to simultaneously manage concurrent processes, hence its ability to execute more than one task at the same time. This permits real-time runs of more than one *virtual console,* timing the activities and synchronizing the processes. This faculty will eventually be necessary for—and therefore characterize— the advanced workstations, making it possible to use one's own PC to write a letter on one video while the second shows the results of a query, and the third shows a graphic presentation.

In terms of *concurrent presentation* as contrasted to concurrent processing, the OS requires a multifunction real-time monitor (RTM) for process dispatching. The dispatcher

selects a waiting process of higher priority,

suspends a process in execution,

traps the data, and

returns the suspended process on CPU availability.

Such activities underline the wisdom of incorporating a hard disc in the PC for program storage, if not for data.

The projected need for concurrent processing induced Microsoft to develop the MS DOS Release 4.0 for late 1984. Release 4.0 features a merger of the basic features of this OS with those of Xenix (the Microsoft-designed Unix choice). This will allow the software manufacturer not to have to translate every horizontal or vertical software program for every OS which it supports. It will also open new avenue in OS design.

The coming years may prove the really major competitor of both CPM and MS DOS is Unix and its clones. Xenix is now available on the 8086, 68000 and Z8000 microprocessors. It will be handy for Microsoft to have only one OS for which to target horizontal software developments. (Let's add that today the typical MS DOS Release 2.0 is not necessarily compatible with PC DOS Release 2.0 on the IBM PC.

Differences exist in user visibility and functionality. The IBM PC has additional utilities such as tree routine, mode command, and disc compare utility not necessarily available on other PCs running MS DOS.)

Toward Integrated Software

At the same time that more emphasis is being placed on OS by the leading manufacturers, other software vendors are promising *integrated software*. Thus, different programs work in similar and familiar ways; saving a disc file or erasing a line is always the same. Integrated packages can either consist of a collection of programs running independently, or appear to be one big program running under a single-task operating system.

Whether any one integrated package will have sufficiently strong individual components to justify widespread use, only time will tell. Just the same, the market will define for which PC integrated software will be written.

This is one of several issues involved in the proliferation of IBM clones as many companies introduce compatible micros. Yet, strict compatibility is illegal: The clones cannot reproduce IBM's copyrighted read only memory (ROM). As a result, some of the software won't run on the clones, though most IBM-targeted software will run on the better compatible micros. That is why it is wise to try out every program first, using discs prepared for an IBM PC. Some software vendors try to get their programs to run on every possible machine; the most important software firms are concentrating on the IBM PC. For the incompatible micros, the software delay is running high—up to a large fraction of the machine's lifetime.

Quite surprisingly, some traditional computer companies display little understanding of the micro market. One item from a major vendor uses CPM 86 as its main operating system, but buyers get no disc formatting program. This company planned to sell preformatted discs at more than twice the going rate to a captive audience. Because it also needed to protect its other products, the company chose to support weak word processing software for its PC. Potential buyers who ask for something better are directed to a different computer, the old-fashioned word processor unit.

Another firm, predominantly a WP manufacturer, found itself with a new micro far more powerful than its traditional word processing product selling for less than half the price. To protect the profits from its established lines, this vendor weakened the word processing program on its PC.

Companies following such policies are at best near-sighted. They tend to miss the key point that *the biggest payoff is likely to come in the field of office automation.* The key to the future office productivity and decision support market will be computerized networks that switch messages between computer terminals, telephones and other office equipment. All will be consolidated into a WS on a desk.

Also near-sighted are software developments which rest on languages of a questionable future. It is, for instance, said that applications in Basic are transportable between different microprocessor types while supporting an equal file format on disc. Is it rational, though, to develop new applications in Basic?

The compatibility concept through a software bus is good and can be extended beyond a specific OS. For instance, based on the "C" language and a run time library (RTL), Digital Research brings its environment applications developed for Unix and other OS.

The last reference should retain considerable attention. As operating systems become generic, the choice of language is the next important milestone. Let's look at this development:

1. An operating system is introduced for a specific class of products.
2. Users come to recognize it as easier to be implemented.
3. Once implementation is no more the challenge, efficiency and more power become the criterion for choice.
4. The same is true of versatility addressing many environments.

By now, users prefer to buy a generic OS because they want the ability to move or share software among various brands of computers. Unix has a predominance because of the reasons outlined in references 2, 3, and 4. Developed by Bell Laboratories on a microcomputer, Unix is today the most sophisticated of the generic operating systems. It has been broadly used for educational purposes under a special low-cost licensing agreement with colleges and universities.

Unix is written in the "C" language, and this improves its portability among hardware engines. It also features valid supports. There are an estimated 300 utilities including database management, photocomposition interfaces, various communications capabilities and word processing. Unix supports both fixed and variable length records. With its flexible communications capability, it can serve as a good frontend for distributed information systems.

Unet is an example of the software fitting this reference. This is a software communications product for networking Unix and Unix-based systems. As such it provides the possibility to simultaneously establish multiple interactive links between different types of computers. Linked PCs may be physically adjacent or geographically distributed and interconnected in any desired topology. They can use a variety of physical links (RS-232, RS-449, LAN interfaces) and interconnect different systems, matching the right computer configuration to each task.

Unet uses a vendor independent internet protocol (IP) and transmission control protocol (TCP) developed by ARPA and adopted as a standard by the Department of Defense. Remote file transfer gives users the ability to efficiently transfer ASCII or binary files between computers in the network. Virtual terminal facilities allow users to access the full power of a remote system as if they were directly connected to that system. An automatic routing capability assures that all network services are provided transparently through intermediate nodes. Process-to-process communication provides users with the ability to link their programs with others running concurrently on other computers in the network.

Finally, electronic mail facilities permit users to send mail to and receive mail from any computer in the network. Though this is not precisely an integrated software offering, as far as communications are concerned it has many integrated software features.

Unix also supports Ingres, a relational database management system, but perhaps a better example of OS-DBMS integrated functions is Oasis. This is a general-purpose OS for 8-BPW and 16-BPW microcomputers. It runs on various computers, provides ease of use, and reduces many of the tedious tasks that are ordinarily part of program development and execution.

Like Unix, Oasis was programmed primarily in the "C" language. Both a central memory-resident and a disc-resident, it retrieves program transients needed for a particular operation from the disc. It requires approximately 20K of memory and up to 500K of auxiliary storage.

Above all, Oasis is a database management OS for microcomputers which (like CPM) originated with the 8-BPW processors.

The Oasis Basic language aids in program development have editing, interpreting, and debugger facilities. This OS combines the advantages of an interpreter and a compiler; the user can make changes to the source program and immediately execute it again. As the language is compiled, programs are processed faster, memory requirements are reduced, and the source program is protected.

In terms of database management, Oasis supports file input and output to the oneline disc drives, console printers, and so on. It handles the following file access methods:

direct, random by relative record number,

indexed, random by key,

absolute, and

relocatable.

It also permits up to 16 data files to be allocated or opened within a program and used simultaneously.

Though this OS was originally designed for standalone machines, it does provide some communications capability: sending and receiving files in batch mode and permitting the hardware to act as a terminal to another computer. The 2780 and 3780 binary synchronous protocols have been added, supporting transmission speeds of 1.2 to 9.6 KBPS.

As far as internal operations are concerned, Oasis offers up to eight levels of job priority scheduling. The system also offers interprogram communication, allowing commonly used programs to be stored in central memory, thus eliminating program load delays.

Chapter 9

DBMS FOR MICROCOMPUTERS

Introduction

Database management systems for microcomputers will become more prominent when truly distributed databases are implemented, even if we handle large databases at one central site. As mainframes and micros start to communicate in a steady, properly planned manner, the need for DBMS increases.

Most DBMS applications are created specifically for the purpose of sharing data, and though the PC, by definition, is not meant to be shared, the text and data which it accesses and manipulates is a shared resource.

Micro costs help promote micro-DBMS usage. If costs had been high, DBMS would have been cost-justified on computers large enough to process many transactions. However, micro-DBMS costs are only 2% to 3% of those for large systems, and their sophistication is high.

In a certain sense, we can contrast database management systems as being implemented on microcomputers and on mainframes. For the former, software publishers have come up with solutions in which attention has been focused on simplifying the inquiry and data entry procedures. We are also seeing better integration of software products than before. An example is the ability to extract data from a database and incorporate them into text being prepared with word processing software.

What really constitutes a DBMS? The best way to look at it is as a complete set of products, including:

data definition facilities

data manipulation tools

a data directory

a file manager

telecommunications management

means for querying the database

tools for producing reports

transaction and updating capabilities

journaling, and so on.

These products, including data dictionaries that control the environment, constitute DBMS. Yet, terminology is a basic problem as vendors attempt to offer a single, comprehensive DBMS solution for all needs, including applications programming and maintenance.

Whether we talk of mainframe or micro-based systems, the DBMS is an integrated set of tools to handle all data requirements. This is far from the late 1960s/early 1970s when people thought of a DBMS as a data manipulation and data definition language capability, plus a set of utilities. Now, though, users are looking for a whole series of integrated tools that include not only classical DBMS functions but also functional means to enhance the workstation. A DBMS is a storage and retrieval facility for formatted data, and is an important means to support data sharing among multiple applications.

The critical question on whether or not to use a micro-DBMS should be answered in a factual manner by specifying the degree to which it helps run a database: from the viewpoint of daily usage to the implementation of dictionary services, database management perspectives, and its maintenance.

A valid DBMS applied at the local database level provides query tools and a wide range of reliability and recovery features. It promotes database security that protects against improper or unauthorized access. The DBMS must have the capacity to acquire, manipulate, and report information to the user needs in a useful format. In that sense, the DBMS can be seen as a single-application system aimed at the end-user.

DBMS in a Distributed Database Environment

At the microcomputer level, text and data move out of the mainframe and mini into the workplace. This makes us recognize that we need tools to move data in, out and around. That's the first reason why a micro-DBMS can help.

We know that as the DP/DB/DC environment gets distributed, we need efficient tools to locate data. The prerequisite is the setting of a guiding principle: Text and data should be logically in one place, but *physically* it should be distributed in many places and support media.

When we work in the area of a true distribution of text and data, we must examine:

redundancy

resiliency

commitment

versatility

synchronization

expandability

journalization

recovery

security

integrity.

To a significant extent, these requirements are interrelated. Whether a failure occurs or a node crashes or an access is repeated, the system must be able to back the transaction to the commitment point. This is no different than what we have been doing with big machines, but in a networking environment we would gladly let the PC be an extension of the mainframe.

At the same time, on a LAN we would like to assure minimum record-locking to allow two PCs to share the same file. A similar statement can be made of applications programming. In fact, integrated software tools such as Lotus 1-2-3 and the Lisa programs do incorporate some functional routines with typical DBMS services. Such practice can be expected to expand during the coming years.

A DBMS is required when several independent applications need to access the same data. Since each application program has a different view of the data, the DBMS helps reformat the IE to satisfy these views. The DBMS also protects parts of the data against access by unauthorized programs.

In a PC implementation, data control requirements can be too costly to justify for a single program. A properly chosen DBMS can meet the need of separating data handling from application programming. It keeps track of whether the data are in a core, on a sequential file, a direct file, an indexed file, or wherever, leaving the application programs unchanged. When we want to access our files for a given application, the application program does not need to intervene. The DBMS does the job. It also enables the creation of different files, enlarging the means of expression.

As experience with truly distributed systems at the WS level starts coming in, we begin to appreciate that the lack of microfiles has been the fault of the first generation of PCs. This fault is now in the process of being corrected—but at the same time experience suggests

the ability to integrate heterogenous systems,

a better use of the LAN bandwidth than the transport of repetitive programs or data, and

the need to allow the same view of data.

Each of these points is a good reason for a micro-DBMS. The decision as to which DBMS to install, when considered as part of a data management program, should be based on a view of the database as a methodology evaluating the merits of a DBMS for a given installation. Thus, the technical characteristics of the product become the primary consideration in selecting the micro-DBMS. But there is a prerequisite— to allow for an exposure of the database concept at all levels in the organization, as well as for a true commitment to the programs to be made.

Selection criteria must evidently account for the fact that many micro-DBMS (and some mini-DBMS) do not include data dictionaries or natural language frontends. (The latter are considered to be the most useful features of mainframe DBMS.)

This leads to the thought (advanced by some specialists) that the very idea of a DBMS is antithetical to the way micros typically are used: They say that DBMS allow users to share data, that micros are often standalone machines, and that micro databases are rarely large enough to justify a DBMS. This argument is, however, weakened when we talk of local area databases which are large in comparison with personal microfiles. Indeed, a growing number of specialists consider that micros are powerful enough to handle many tasks that were formerly assigned to more capacious machines, and conclude that

micro-DBMS will have a vital role to play as the size and cost of powerful hardware shrink;

users will continue to demand more of their own computing power; and

networks of micros soon will be handling many large tasks.

The services to be rendered in such an environment will be that much more effective when a functional upgrade is implemented both in the services provided by a DBMS in a LAN and in the way the service is packaged and delivered.

Today, in many instances a WS is designed around a display and keyboard provided for a particular application. In distributed processing, it has capacity for, say, screen formatting and editing. The DBMS should be able to handle all text and data functions beyond these vertical applications-oriented routines.

The future of micro-DBMS promises networked databases, calling up any piece of information we need. The system will be able to search through linked databases for files, with mainframes and minis tied into this scheme. This is another reason why the arrival of mainframe-style DBMS for micros is an exciting development.

The new DBMS promise to give users unprecedented computer power. Most vendors are developing new features and options for the microcomputer versions of their DBMS. With LAN, micro-DBMS are expected to tie larger numbers of users into comprehensive networks; for instance, MDBS has been linked to the Ungermann-Bass network.

These considerations bring the DBMS issue under a new light. To appreciate this reference, let's recall that all commercially successful database systems developed in the 1960s and 1970s were designed to satisfy the needs of a centralized data processing function. It is therefore quite reasonable that new products for small machines should not be clones of these earlier systems.

Design-wise, the natural response seems to be that only a subset is required. In fact, the opposite is true. The micro-DBMS must provide more services than the current generation of mainframe DBMS—and it should do so in a flexible, expandable manner.

A Growing Awareness

The growing awareness of the need for DBMS is a need for integrated nonprocedural languages, dictionary control validation, text/data integrity and maintenance, and the ability to handle graphics in the database, among other reasons.

Another reason is security. Even without a distributed database, an increasing number of employees have access to corporate data resources. Is there enough security provided so that only authorized personnel can access the data? The answer can only then be *yes* if through software and hardware tools we are able to implement security at the user level.

Passwords that let users access only certain files are one example. Another method is through the PC so that only certain files and data can be sent to a specific WS. A third approach is security implemented at the file level.

Several different security levels can be used to protect a given IE. The weakest link in database security is the lack of integrity controls and balances to reconcile the contents of the database. Security in a DBMS involves:

assured authorized access only

protected data integrity

recovery and restart capabilities

encryption (if necessary)

elimination of data redundancy

controlled I/O.

As a result of these and other facilities, the system allows the user to bring up his programs much faster. Also, applications programs are then only concerned with IE manipulation—leaving placement and retrieval to the DBMS.

In terms of database integrity, the DBMS assists the application in maintaining data integrity by providing automatic range checking and other facilities. Check summing can be provided for database pages. Just as helpful is the logging system and recovery utility.

Data encryption, password protection, and access code facilities permit control over a user's read or write access to IE. Ranges for items can be specified at the database definition stage and verified at the time of data input, with check summing performed on demand.

Users become aware that control of a distributed database makes feasible a faster access, reaching directly any record. The proper DBMS can also minimize the content of a DDB by locking users out of sections. All parts don't need to be online at the same time.

A different way of making this statement is that in a low level file management system we may have to open several files at the same time. With DBMS we open a file only once and what the applications need to know is:

1. Record type name
2. Set type name
3. Relationship between record type
4. Item type (numeric data, alphabetic, etc.)

Changes related to this manipulation will be consistent. Also, the DBMS commands prove to be of great help in data management—in many cases, about 20 commands out of a range serving 90% of all applications. This is particularly true of a distributed environment with job-oriented database sections.

What is a truly distributed DBMS? It is one that allows the data to be located as close to the end-user as possible to satisfy information requirements at his most localized processor. It tends to be directory driven so that users can access IE from any location within the organization without having to know where it came from. (This is another issue of security.)

This is the theoretical definition; now the practical one as of 1985. The adoption by Project *Athena* at MIT of Unix 4.2 BSD (Berkeley Software Distribution) brought under perspective the role demons play in a truly distributed environment. Demons are network-wide supervisory processes. They are defined to respond to specific situations that arise during processing and file handling.

Born when a process is created anywhere in the network, demons watch registers, indexes, values, etc. for indication they are needed. A truly distributed DBMS needs demons, but none currently supports them.

In this environment, one of the DBMS functions will do transaction logging, allowing the creation of sequential log files with preimages, going to the backup copy to a central (or regional backup) database. This is particularly necessary if we plan to use the DBMS to bring office automation and data processing together.

Another reason for promoting a distributed DBMS is program portability. Software development is expensive and labor-intensive. With a higher degree of portability, the benefits of investment in applications programming can be magnified by transporting application systems across a wide range of micro environments. A result of portability is a uniform, standardized approach of applications development.

Figure 9.1 presents a basic structure for multiple functionality to be implemented within a LAN environment with user-friendly WS attached to the network. As different applications programs address the same text and database, the DBMS automatically maintains data in sorted orders which can include sorting by as many data items as the user desires. Memory can be managed using demand paging virtual memory techniques. To minimize storage requirements needed to run a given application, portions of the DBMS can be selectively

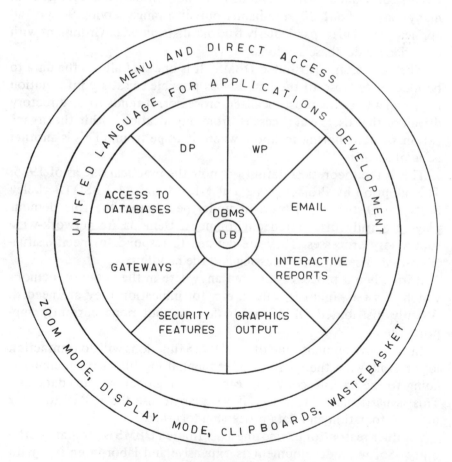

Figure 9.1

linked to the application software. This means that an application developer has to keep in memory only that portion of the system actually used by a program.

While such features are not available in all micro-DBMS, and when available they can be selectively implemented, an equally vital subject is the choice of the first applications. It is good to start with an application that is fairly self-contained but still part of something larger. This is part of a policy of establishing a strategic plan for developing a true database system within a distributed environment.

Relational, Networking, and Hierarchical Structures

One of the data management issues to be decided is whether the databases are going to be primarily static or dynamic in terms of their content. This will help decide which sort of algorithm should be chosen.

Relational DBMS are more appropriate for dynamic situations where the relationships between pieces of information are likely to change. An hierarchical or a network system may be better suited to larger applications drawn from a relatively static database.

We will see in the following discussion that each architecture has its own advantages, though end-users don't really know what the system's structure is—and they don't care. All they want is to be able to do their queries and reports and get the information they need.

The reason why this issue is important to the system specialist is that the type of structure can make a big difference in the initial design time required and in the future flexibility of the system. Relational structures can be more user-friendly, though the preparatory work is somewhat more involved.

A relational database is a collection of IE arranged in columns and rows. Setting up this database involves the creation and filing of the tables with pertinent data. To expand it, we add new tables without rewriting existing application programs.

The major advantage of relational databases is their simplicity. They are easy to design, modify, and maintain, and allow for easily locating information. These advantages are readily apparent if we compare the operations necessary for other types of database organization to a relational structure.

A relational database does not require physical pointers or extra linkage records. Each file may contain megabytes or gigabytes and have a couple of hundred access keys. Data is topologically independent, and files can be linked dynamically at run time to form new relationships. Once we set up and profile the database, the operating system automatically takes care of data access and file locating activities.

A relational system tends to give cleaner, faster insight into the management and manipulation of data. There is a growing agreement among DBMS experts that relational systems are easier to use, make programmers more productive, and provide more data independence than the network or hierarchical systems.

The main criticism of these systems is that their performance has not been very good for some production applications, probably because relational technology is new. However, there is no inherent reason why a relational DBMS cannot be as fast as a network or hierarchical system.

At one time, users were also concerned about the amount of main memory the DBMS required. This is no more an often-heard reference. What is heard is that there are applications the user needs to look at a customer, his orders, and the items on an order, and this resembles an hierarchical approach. However, the user may need to look directly to a file record or from one file to another, and this requires a network method. If he wants information on all the orders for a specific date, he will be better served by the relational method.

Relational systems are well-suited to query-oriented, multikey retrieval. Relational DBMS can handle cases supported by some kind of index, but they don't provide structure where structure already exists. Network and hierarchical systems can, where structure does exist, offer more efficiency than relational systems, but a relational system gives some independence where structures are fluid and users need immediate access.

Figure 9.2 identifies the IE in a given database as being grouped into three large implementation areas: clients, factories, and suppliers. Each has its own subgroupings or clusters. A relational approach arranges these clusters in a matrix-oriented form. The same clusters grouped in a networking mode lead to many pointers (Figure 9.3), while the hierarchical approach creates a decreasing flexibility as the tree structure, reflecting the hierarchy, grows.

To repeat, there are basically three approaches to database structure: hierarchical, network, and relational. The hierarchical structure is an organization with data arranged in ascending order. Any lower

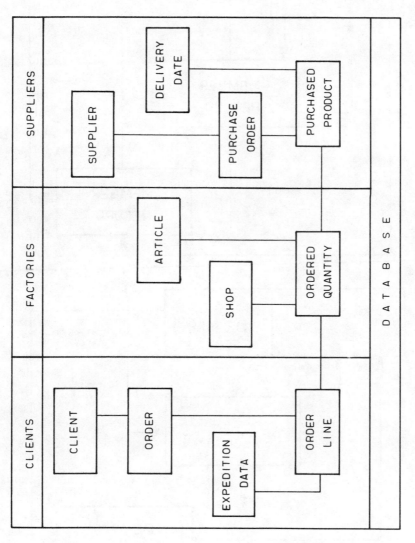

Figure 9.2

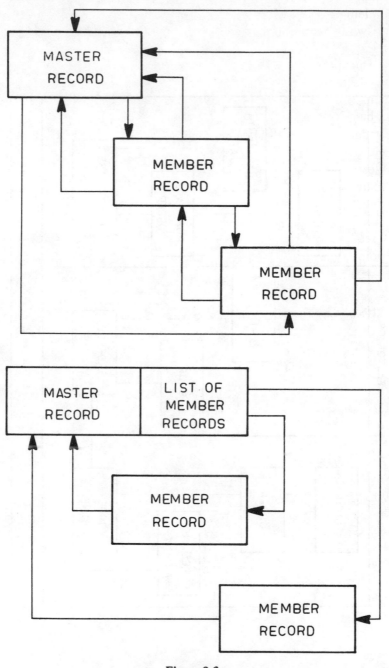

Figure 9.3

level element can be connected directly to only one higher level element, which immediately poses a problem: how to design and organize data.

The problem is that this decision, made in the early development stage, determines the future performance and expandability of the system. Since each record has only one owner or parent, records often must be duplicated for accessibility.

As databases get larger, we have major updating problems. The second design issue concerns deletions. If we delete a record, we also risk destroying the secondary records under it because there no longer is a logical path to those records.

A network database structure permits multiple parent records, but linked by pointers or physical disc addresses. Changing an order, deleting a record, or moving data around means changing and reconnecting the pointers. This leads to constant and considerable maintenance.

The Rearend Engine

A rearend processor is a specialized engine whose primary function is to offload the main processor. Though the history of such machines is still short, many experts feel that they have a potential. If we can perform many of the functions in hardware, then we can obtain better results.

To start with, a main advantage hardware provides is speed, but it does not offer flexibility when we try to improve our technology. On the other hand, we are moving increasingly into networking, and this makes the database machine more attractive.

In a networking environment, we no longer have to attach the database to any particular processor, but can put it on the network as a service (that is, as a file server). This way, the WS can be connected to it quickly and inexpensively.

These references identify design objectives of database processors. A more ambitious feature is to establish relationships between stream-oriented files and record-oriented files. Such information may coexist in the same database. Typically, in executing its functions, the database engine will provide intelligent file services to other machines connected to the LAN. To perform its duty, it will be positioned as a high level building block.

A network can have separate databases, offering the ability for any program in the network to access any one of them, or it may feature a single database with parts of it distributed across many computers.

Host-to-database engine communication must be sufficiently rich to accommodate independent conversations between the engine and multiple applications residing in different WS; the deployment of database servers in a network; and extensive error detection and correction capabilities.

The messages a WS sends to a rearend engine may actually be encoded sequences of commands for defining, manipulating and administering data. Hence, this engine can be regarded as a functionally comprehensive relational DBMS, supporting an active data dictionary, manipulation through set-oriented operators, and control through a variety of integrity, security, and recovery mechanisms. Set operators are essential to minimize the communication between a host and database engine. Traffic is further reduced through a macro facility permitting any frequently used sequences of commands to be catalogued as one unit.

Database sharing by multiple online users can be provided through a multitasking executive interleaving command execution, a file system that coordinates concurrent access to stored data, and a recovery mechanism guaranteeing the application of sequences of updates or other types of accesses. To be implemented at the PC level, such systems should have board level components. It should allow users to slide a board into a microcomputer with hard disc and gain database capabilities immediately. Alternatively, in a LAN environment, it must make feasible the addition of sophisticated database capabilities to the network.

An Example at the Microfile Level

We said that a micro-DBMS is justified as the local database (LDB) level, and less so in running a microfile. While this reference may change with time as hard disc costs drop and WS files become increasingly larger, today the handling of microfiles calls for file management routines rather than DBMS.

Let's see what these routines can do. As an example, we will take a novel approach to the management of microfiles particularly oriented to office chores—the Personal Filing System (PFS, marketed by Software Publishing Corporation).

This software works like a paper filing system, enabling its user to record, file, retrieve, and to summarize information. The package also enables him to organize his information on forms he designs himself on the computer screen. Once he has created the basic form (with spaces for all the necessary data) all he need do is fill in the blanks. He can enter data in any order and the package takes care of finding the information when he needs it. After he has filled in the form, he can store it on a floppy for future use.

If the user does not like the form he originally designed, the package lets him change just the form without having to totally reenter the information on it. The user can find specific characters, words, names, or numbers; he can also instantly update by typing in the new information, or print it with a few simple keystrokes. He can even print selected items in sorted order, such as a mailing list.

An extension routine provides reporting facilities. To do so, it uses the information on the forms already established to give the user a report structure helping him to spot trends, to make plans, and to make decisions more effectively.

Once he has his information stored in the PFS file, the user can summarize it in a variety of ways:

sort by article number;

compute the value of each item in inventory;

list employees and their qualifications;

sort by salary;

list revenues and expenses subtotaled by class;

compute balance.

This routine will sort, calculate, total, format and print presentation-quality reports with automatic centering.

Chapter 10

VERY HIGH LEVEL LANGUAGES

Introduction

The implementation examples outlined in this chapter bring into focus a whole new perspective in computer programming. Collectively, the new tools are known as very high level languages (VHLL) or, also, fourth generation languages.

We all know that during the last decade hardware has changed tremendously—becoming more compact but also more powerful, low cost and widespread. The capable use of these new tools calls for abandoning "traditional" concepts and images. It also requires both management guidance and specialist training.

Efficient results cannot be obtained by anything less than a polyvalent approach to the implementation of new hardware and software technologies. If we fail to account with value-added capabilities in computers and communications, we will only carry the costs. There will be small benefits to reap.

This is the basic message as we study fourth generation programming languages, and the computer market votes with dollars. As projected in early 1986, the growth patterns are:

	Yearly Percent Increase
1. Software	30%
2. Communications	25%
3. Hardware	15%
4. Staff	8%
5. Supplies	7%

Such percentages are quite significant. By 1989, the computer market is expected to reach $125 billion. In other terms, over 200% the $60 billion of 1985 (out of a total high technology expenditure of about $115 billion).

Hardware-wise, a large share will go to PC. But it is the software component which will steal the show—from DBMS to horizontal software, fourth generation languages and expert systems.

Fourth Generation Programming Languages

Significant productivity gains require an integrated, uninterrupted effort, continuous personnel training, and initiatives in several implementation areas. A software productivity improvement program can have a large payoff, but this calls for sustained action and commitment.

Tools alone are of limited value if other factors do not contribute to this goal. Programmer productivity has four components:

1. Motivation
2. Computer-based tools
3. Efficient learning of the new methodology
4. Intelligent WS support at each desk.

It is relatively easy for programmers to know how to use the new programming tools—if they want to. Through the features of fourth generation languages, developers can produce thousands of lines of code in a small fraction of the time Cobol requires. Also important is the fact that better development tools improve motivation. The object of a VHLL is to provide a fast, versatile and intelligently organized programming system to save programming time, eliminating the need for a large staff of computer specialists; upgrading the capabilities of those experts already in the employment of the firm; and coinvolving the user—thus saving future incomprehensions and frictions.

Fourth generation languages fall into different categories, each with its own advantages. A valid way to distinguish them is in the following five classes:

1. Spreadsheet-type systems
2. Database management and query
3. Productivity-oriented languages

4. New programming languages
   artificial intelligence
   graphics

5. Programming extensions to the OS and special
   software capabilities.

Some of these classes both complement and overlap one another. File management-oriented languages offer some spreadsheet capabilities, while both database-type coding and spreadsheets provide some computing routines.

Let's now see what is supported by each of the aforementioned five classes by way of functionality and programming routines.

Spreadsheet systems were originally devised by Daniel Bricklin as a calculations aid with simultaneous update capabilities. However, spreadsheets are now also user-friendly programming tools.

VisiCalc has had so far more than two dozen clones. It has also led to *integrated software,* which means multiple applications in one package. For example, Lotus 1-2-3 is really four programs operating under a common command structure: a calc program, a graphics program, a word processor, and a database program. Such evolution has been largely characterized by database facilities built upon the spreadsheet concept.

While the most important contribution of integrated software is its integrated ability for diverse programs, some current trends include:

the ability to name entries,

assigning a name to a worksheet area,

referring to that name when entering formulas,

linking worksheets, and

providing a multiwindowing capability.

Desq, Vision, Star, and Lisa are examples of *multiwindowing.* However, to support multiwindow capabilities and other features, we need a high resolution screen and added power through the new microprocessors (such as Intel's 80286 and 80386 and Motorola's 68010 and 68020). The same references are valid for moving the cursor between windows, overlaying, zooming, and rotating. As we will see, this also leads to graphics capabilities.

The second major class of VHLL is *database management and query systems*. The new generation of DBMS query facilities is typically relational in nature, involving a sophisticated command file and being reasonably fast. Such systems are the forerunners of a new generation of OS which will integrate the classical monitor functions with databasing, query, and transaction processing.

> *Transactional* systems guide the terminal and, through it, the end-user.
>
> A *query* system is typical of an *interactive* environment where the end-user guides the system. The user can create his own menu, has the ability to write command files with conditional branching, and can access any IE in the database without knowing its address. The user can interact with the delivery system through a scenario simulation, and can also use various types of input as long as they are acceptable to the machine.

This makes the DBMS/query aggregate a powerful tool, though not necessarily as easy to use by nonprofessionals as the spreadsheet. It therefore appeals, to end-users for example, learned in comptuer science.

As an example, Ingres—originally designed as a relational DBMS—has recently evolved into a powerful programming language due to the following eight features:

1. QUEL. This is the kernel of the language structure used to retrieve and update IE in the database. It works through VHLL statements.

2. QBF provides query-type interactive video presentations. Hence, it permits the end-user to guide the system—which is typical of an interactive environment.

3. VIFRED provides visual form definition. It helps define the form (screen) which will be used with QBF. (QBF does not permit modifications to the full screen or menu.)

4. RW is a complete report writer allowing word processing, electronic publishing, and so on.

5. RBF is a report-by-form structure that is easy to manipulate by the end-user.

6. EQUEL (embedded QUEL in "C" programs) makes feasible the use of very high level commands by Ingres within a "C" program by means of a processor. Idem for defined forms.

7. ABF is a form manipulation and presentation language similar to QUEL/EQUEL, but at a much higher level. It is mainly transactional because the end-user is guided by the system.

8. GBF is a graphics-by-form language which integrates with the other Ingres subsets to offer a complete graphics facility.

The object of *productivity-oriented languages* is to offer a comprehensive, easy-to-manipulate approach to the answer of programming needs. These languages are complete structured systems for producing not only lines of code but also full documentation.

Documentation is kept by the computer and is updated automatically by the machine while the programmer changes an instruction, redefines a table, alters its contents, adds, modifies, or deletes. Such operations regard all records handled by the language. Yet, productivity-oriented languages may be a passing species overtaken by the data-base programming languages.

New programming languages are different than those existing in terms of usage and implementation. They are typically efficiency-oriented and designed to fit a given need within the broadening range of applications requirements.

Artificial intelligence and graphics are two specific examples of new programming images.

A language often discussed for *artificial intelligence* is Prolog. Among languages designed for dataflow machines are ID and Valid.

Prolog is basically a procedural programming language to solve goals sequentially. For a given goal, it searches to find a clause whose head can be made to match the goal. If the clause is an implication then it, in turn, attempts to solve the subgoals. The possible result of a goal will be failure or success, plus possible values associated with variables.

To achieve success for a goal, all the subgoals must succeed. If one of the subgoals cannot be solved, Prolog backtracks and tries to find another clause whose head matches the goal. If no untried clauses remain, then the failure is returned for the goal.

Languages for *graphics* applications typically include drawing aids and the ability to add already designed charts. Such languages do not require on the user's behalf any special systems knowledge to utilize the high resolution screen to its fullest capacity.

Graphics languages have:

built-in editors,

calculation routines for diagram details,

the ability to output among three different graphic machines (screen, plotter, printer),

headlines, dates and explanatory texts,

scaling capabilities and the division of axes of reference.

The desired diagram is defined in the dialog, the input being done through functional commands. The result is available on the screen and can be changed in an interactive manner.

Stored in files, graphics are callable at any time. The design validation process, full debugging aids and other tools are included within a package. We can think of a given character as being a small window which will be transferred to the specific screen.

There are similarities between this new generation of languages and database programming systems. Both operate on data, with calculation a subsidiary activity. Also, they both tend to show relational characteristics.

The fifth class of new programming languages is characterized by the *merger of programming features with the operating system.* For all OS, we need databasing, datacomm and flow control to be really effective. (A similar statement can be made of programming capability.)

There are benefits to be obtained by merging the features of OS, DBMS and programming structures. A four-party integration can best be appreciated in the Unix-Shell-Ingres-"C" language reference.

Another example of programming extensions to the OS and special software capabilities is IBM's ADF. ADF modules:

permit reading messages from a terminal;

implement segment layout rules;

retrieve segments from the database;

apply handling rules;

update IE in the database;

provide the logic for processing segments;

input transaction rules; and

write messages to a terminal.

Like the other VHLL currently available, this type of language works through menus and options.

While some OS languages are often discussed as transaction drivers, they offer significantly greater capabilities to users. Most vital is a great improvement in programmer productivity.

Programmers' Productivity Through a 4GL

Fourth generation languages are very high level as compared to Cobol, Fortran and others born in the 1950s and 1960s. Moreover, they offer facilities needed for today's sophisticated environment in computers and communications.

For a quarter century, Fortran was *the* scientific language, but it is not structured, has no string manipulation, no inherent databasing capability, and no graphics primitives. Yet, these are fundamental needs in a present-day engineering and scientific environment. A similar statement can be made of Cobol in regard to business applications.

A modern VHLL permits working easily with a number of applicative products at one time, such as screen design, procedural evaluation, applications programming, and database management. It offers a well-structured common interface to all applications needs; ensures that man-information communications characteristics are uniformly applied to all of the users' applications; and integrates these applications under a common work environment. If properly used, a VHLL assures much greater productivity for the professional systems expert. It also allows the nonprofessional to program the computer, albeit at a lesser level of sophistication.

The level of a programming language is determined by the power of the semantic primitives which it supports.

> Commands provided by lower level (or obsolete "high level") languages lie closer to the elementary operations implemented by the hardware.

> A higher level of programming presupposes primitives with storage allocation and control structures.

> A still higher level supports more abstract but also more powerful operations, manipulating entire arrays.

Depending on their level of implementation, programming languages can provide very high level abstract objects and operations on them, as well as high level control structures. Such programming styles can simplify the programmer's task by eliminating large amounts of relatively routine detail that would otherwise have to be supplied.

Given these characteristics and the documented productivity ratios which we will review in the following paragraphs, the best advice is that the major quantity of the work to be done in computer programming should be based on a VHLL. Only a minor quantity of computer programming should be handled through so-called "high level" languages which date back to the 1950s.

The simplification of the programmer's task and the simultaneous manipulation of objects through the language's own primitives are the two pillars on which rests the very much higher *programmer's productivity*. In a VHLL like dBase II, some 50 HLL instructions can be replaced by one command. This, plus an agile file, is behind the fact that some three man-months of Cobol programming can be done in one man-day with dBase II.

One example of programmer productivity through dBase II is a purchasing application. It involved a main program and 20 subprograms. The total represented 70% of the manual work in a company's purchasing department. This project required 10 man-days of dBase II programming. Management estimated that had classical programming approaches been followed they would have required 80 man-days of system analysis and 200 man-days of programming. Also necessary would have been time for installing the system and adjusting the main database to the application.

A second example is an order handling and statistics application. It involved one main program and 15 subprograms, including all report formats. The total time necessary with dBase II was 12 man-days of work, whereas Cobol programming would have required 25 times more effort. Had this work been done on mainframe, it would have been necessary to work out a complicated access to the database. This was so involved that, if executed, it would have brought the ratio to 1:50.

There is also a structural delay issue to be accounted for. It takes a few days to get an application on PC, and it may take months or years to get something from a mainframe.

Still another application used datacomm software to transfer from central information files to the PC and for reporting purposes. This application was made by a manufacturer's shipping department using dBase II and PCTS (personal computer transfer system).

Being a program and therefore a file, dBase II can be stored on the file server of a mainframe and downloaded to the workstations. However, if the applications programs are written in this language, it is necessary to have it at each WS in a resident fashion.

In Norway, one savings bank wanted a new program. Programming on a mainframe through APL was estimated to take 10 man-months of work (programming only). Weary of such delays, a young banker got a PC and, through Multiplan, did the needed program in one day.

Multiplan is a spreadsheet. As such, it particularly appeals to the person with no experience in computers. Through Multiplan, the end-user also saved his bank a lot of money: running one online terminal with APL is very expensive.

In Germany, on an IBM 3081, APL consumed 70% of the computer power for applications which—when restudied—were able to go on supermicro. This is still another aspect of the microcomputer revolution.

In evaluating spreadsheet vs. Cobol in terms of programmer productivity, computer experts were asked to estimate the time necessary to program the following three applications:

1. Portfolio management
2. Personnel treasury
3. Current account transactions for home banking

The answers ranged widely for online supports and productivity: 12, 36, 8, 18, 7, 48 man-months of work. Their range was 7 to 48 man-months or 1:6; their average time was 21.5 man-months or 473 man-days.

Yet, these three applications were made in three man-days through Multiplan on a PC—including analysis. Even if the minimum estimate is taken as a reference—seven man-months or 154 man-days—the difference is better than 1:50.

Programming Through Database Languages

Spreadsheets were originally designed for "what if"-type calculations for decision support. It is only recently that spreadsheets and integrated software have become a programming language of excellence, particularly oriented to the end-user.

Something similar can be said of database programming languages such as Ingres, dBase II and DB 2. This class of VHLL evolved from database management systems (DBMS) and became prominent as we slowly came to realize that more than half the time of computer programming is spent with I/O, file design, access, and management.

To properly implement a database programming language, it is absolutely necessary to properly design the *data model*. The end-user cannot do that; the expert programmer should.

Most database programming languages are professional in nature. dBase II from Ashton Tate is such a structure. The more than 50 commands in dBase II are very similar to everyday English. Most of the implementation needs very few commands. Annotations can be shown and changed whenever required.

Two basic characteristics of relational systems are the tabular form in which they are organized and the great flexibility in their usage. Typically, database languages have program generators, menu guidance, and evaluation procedures. The tabular organization facilitates the unexperienced user in his entrance into the system. Each row in a table takes one file which the columns divide into fields. Standard commands facilitate the dialog, the institution of tables, the capture and/or change of data, as well as the search for data based on criteria established by the user. Critical operations, like the combination of several tables into a new table, are done in a way evident to the user.

For recurring usage, selected commands can be collected in files which then guide all processing steps automatically. This results in a safe implementation without detailed systems knowledge by the user, as much of the work is done through menus. However, the more learned the programmer, the more sophisticated the results, as a database language offers:

1. Extended possibilities of file and data treatment: capture, changes, sorting, merging, searching, queries. All usage works on a common data reference which only needs to be captured once and, most importantly, updated only once for all applications.

2. The ability to apply user-defined criteria and automatic selection keys.

3. Built-in mask generators facilitating the development of interactive video screens, including individual headlines.

4. Report generator with schema and content defined in the dialog.

5. Already programmed functional command and menu guidance.

The facilities work interactively and make possible the construction of complete modules, such as financial analysis, general accounting, warehouse management, production planning, and personnel administration. Most important is the fact that these modules have a high portability, provided that the microprocessor-OS infrastructure is compatible and the *same* database language runs on the different systems.

Database programming languages also provide add-ons which further simplify man-machine communication and make the environment more friendly. Ingres, for example, supports QBF, GBF, Vifred, Quel, Equel, RBF, and RW. The add-on of dBase II is the Window of program Tylog. (The Window routine simplifies working with dBase II since it functions as a translator. The user informs the program what he wants to do with dBase II and the dBase Window transforms his requests into the dBase language. It guides the addition, change, search, finding, deletion and printing of database sentences. It makes feasible that functions can be used directly in an existing user program, and also helps in data security and documentation.)

Window supports the addressing and interleaving of more than two databases, but another program—dGraph by Fox & Geller—is the graphics specialist for commercial diagrams, working together with dBase II. DGraph is menu-driven and can be used self-standing or in connection with other routines to make possible a multitude of graphic designs. DGraph

1. Draws diagrams according to direct input or file references calculated from other programs.

2. Changes, completes, or rearranges files through a built-in editor.

3. Automatically calculates diagram details.

4. Secures, edits, and prints diagram definitions.

5. Enriches the diagrams with headlines and explanatory text.

Still another routine that runs under dBase II is the Customer Profitability program by Origin. This is more an applications package than horizontal software, but it also offers some interesting programming commands as we will see below.

Customer Profitability works through menus. In the master frame, selections are:

1. Maintenance
2. Inquiries
3. Processing
4. Reports
5. Installation
6. Exit Application.

For instance, MAINTENANCE refers to the activity which adds, modifies, or deletes data from the files residing in the database. The command ADD inserts new data into the files.

New data refers to that for a new customer rather than new data for an existing customer. A customer is identified by a relationship number.

The command MODIFY changes existing information already stored in the database. Address, branch, and rating can be changed, but other things cannot, such as the relationship number for any customer access.

The command language allows changes only to permitted data. If the user needs to modify the fixed data, he must employ a combination of DELETE and ADD.

The command DELETE puts flags into files indicating that the record no longer is a permanent part of the files. This will remain in the database for some period so that it may be reinstated to permanent status if necessary.

The user can control the period of time by doing a PACK operation. After a PACK is done, the data marked for deletion is physically removed from the files. Prior to that, "deleted" records may be activated.

The command PACK physically removes from the files any records marked for deletion, and recreates index files. The user may want to do this from time to time to reduce storage requirements for the files. However, this does not free up disc space to be used by other files, but rather frees up space within the file to be reused.

Legal and procedural requirements may dictate a time period for which the user must keep historical records, but this can be done in combination with packing the files. A copy of the actual files can be made periodically as a permanent history of the activity.

Finally, the command AUDIT MAINTENANCE reduces the storage requirements for the file on disc. This frees up disc space to be used by other files, deleting the existing empty file and replacing it with a duplicate file of minimal size.

The master menu frame which we have seen is followed by detailed menus. Once Maintenance has been selected, the following is displayed:

1. Control Maintenance
2. Customer Maintenance
3. Relationship Maintenance
4. Account Maintenance
5. Matrix Maintenance
6. Profit Model Maintenance
7. Audit Maintenance

In this frame, the first option is Control Maintenance. This, too, is followed by further details:

1. Processing
2. Legal Lending Limit
3. Year Base
4. Tax Rate
5. Interest Rate
6. Account Type
7. Maturity Type
8. Net Funds Employed
9. Earned Credit
10. Cost of Funds
11. Capital Allocation
12. Administration Cost
13. Acquisition Cost

14. Renewal Cost
15. Transaction Cost
16. Risk Expenses
17. Liquidity Expense
18. Profit Objective

In this frame, selection is 1 through 18. After making a selection, an * will appear beside the selection and the following message will be displayed:

A-Add   M-Modify   D-Delete   P-Pack   *-Exit :-:

The user can then select the desired activity. An * or RETURN key may be entered to return to the Maintenance menu.

This brief example properly documents the user-friendly feature of the facility. The user can examine customers on file, display the information which he requires, establish the relationships he needs, and print the list he chooses. The system itself supports eight key files:

Control identifies what the organization uses to measure profitability.

Control Audit contains images of controls. Anytime Control Maintenance is done—add, modify, delete, activate— an image is created in this file reflecting the activity performed.

Customer identifies individuals and companies that maintain accounts with the organization.

Relationship relates the accounts to the customers.

Relationship Audit contains images of relationships. With Relationship Maintenance, an image is created in this file reflecting the activity performed.

Account is the activity for the accounts.

Matrix contains tables for measuring the activities performed: risk, capital allocation, etc., including cost of funds.

Profit Model contains customer profitability information by month.

The user selects the data he needs, creates his own menus, sets up matrices and matrix lists, verifies data, calculates, and prints account files or quantitative results at his choice.

These examples show that there is a broad range of programming facilities available, from VHLL to horizontal software and even selected vertical routines. The personnel savings that such languages make possible are quite impressive.

At the same time, valid criteria must be established for an intelligent choice. Here is a proposed list:

1. Technical characteristics of the VHLL and available facilities.

2. Programmer productivity to be expressed in lines of code per hour, support for testing and debugging, assistance in documentation, and special tools for the programmer.

3. Compatibility to existing software products for the new applications: personal computers, professional engines, as well as products likely to be acquired.

4. Program maintainability over the life cycle of the routines to be written, with particular emphasis to ease of maintenance and cost.

5. Market support: software companies making available programs with that particular language, survivability of these companies, and overall market drive.

Given the high cost of personnel and the ever-dropping price of computer items, a valid management decision will assign the bulk of the work to be done through a VHLL. This decision should evidently consider the available options, the type of machines to which they apply, and the impact choices may have on the overall effort.

Let's close with the following thought: VisiCalc made the Apple II. Lotus 1-2-3 made the IBM PC. *The fact that microcomputers* are the most versatile personal executive tools *ever invented rests on the key role of commodity software in general, and of spreadsheets/interpreted software in particular.*

This *solution orientation* will be magnified in the coming years. End-users are finally getting the upper hand. In a regional 1985 meeting of the Society for Information Management, an IBM marketing representative was to suggest that *about 80% of the IBM PCs were purchased directly by end-users.* End-users are now sending a clear message to the vendors: "Don't please the bureaucratic central DP organization. Please me."

Chapter 11

EXAMPLES WITH INTEGRATED SOFTWARE AND SPREADSHEETS

Introduction

The goal of this chapter is to help the reader identify salient problems and opportunities of integrated software and spreadsheets.

Many organizations are investing in computers and communications. *If done in the old classical manner* such projects will pose significant personnel requirements in computer specialists. They will consume impressive budgets and overrun their timetables.

Integrated software and spreadsheet programming helps avoid such pitfalls. These programming approaches also open new vistas to the end-user in dealing with his PC.

The coinvolvement of the end-user in instructing his intelligent workstation can solve many problems without personnel increases if the proper retraining, capable direction, and the will to collaborate and apply new technology are present.

We have spoken of the importance of training on PC, integrated software, online access to databases in Chapter 1. If you set up such a program, remember that it is not enough to teach spreadsheet, graphics, and electronic mail. *Computer literacy* involves the ability of people to manage their computer-run files.

Relevant questions are: Do you know how to load-in a file from a disc? how to download files? how to format an information element? how to copy a cell from the spreadsheet? the difference between a value and a label on a spreadsheet? Based on this and other key questions, participants to a course can be assigned according to their learning needs—and invariably there should be updating through additional training.

Most importantly, computer literacy must start at the top management level and proceed top down. The imaginative approach which was started in 1983 by United Technologies by training first of all the most expensive people in the organization, was repeated in 1984 and 1985 by many other organizations. By early 1986, more than 80% of the larger manufacturing firms and financial institutions have given to their senior managers comprehensive hands-on training on the PC.

Integrated Software and Spreadsheet Programming

Integrated software capabilities are primarily targeted toward managers and professionals. Much of their interest centers on:

management planning and control,

financial analysis,

technical planning,

sales and distribution management, and

administrative activities.

With classical DP, a steady change of forms and formats is required. With integrated software and spreadsheets, the same formats can be used. This simplifies procedural changes.

Spreadsheets give fast access to the information the user needs. They allow him to explore the possibilities of that information, enabling him to take into consideration alternative courses of action. This makes the manipulation of planning models easy for the user, consolidating the results, and presenting the information in easy-to-read formats. Training is very simple: In a couple of hours the user should be able to start building his own worksheets, and when he masters the basics, the reference manual will help him build more sophisticated models. The spreadsheet offers him a reference guide which—at the touch of a key—will give him information for the command or function he is using at the moment. When he has found the answer to his question, the user can return to his worksheet where he left off.

VisiCalc, the first spreadsheet available in the market, was born from the observation that many problems are commonly solved with a calculator, a pencil and a sheet of paper. With spreadsheet-type languages, the computer's screen becomes a window which looks upon a much larger memory display.

The user can scroll this window in all four directions to look at any part of the sheet. The spreadsheet is organized as a grid of columns and rows. With Multiplan, one of the best offerings, the rows are numbered 1, 2, 3 ... and so are the columns. The worksheet can be as large as 63 columns wide by 255 rows long. The user can automatically link the pigeonholes created at the intersection; accept data from or feed information into other worksheets; vary the width of the columns to accommodate long words or numbers in one column, shorter ones in the next; and so on.

The spreadsheet accepts lines of text—such as titles—across several columns. At each intersection of a row and column there is a variable with a coordinate identifier:

R1C1 (Row 1, Column 1)
R25C7, and so on.

Into each variable the user can enter one of three types of data: a string, a number, or an arithmetic expression. When the content of a variable is changed, the system automatically recalculates all the other related variables on the sheet. It changes their values and displays them on the screen, if within the window.

Spreadsheets are designed for repetitive work. For instance, if the user employs the COPY command to copy a number six times, the software will remember that. The next time he employs the COPY command, the spreadsheet will propose that he do the same thing. If he does not want to do so, he simply keys in what he wants.

The user can also assign a name, such as PAYROLL or ALGO-RITHM, to an entry or an area of the worksheet, and then refer to that name when entering formulas. On the line he has labeled ALGO-RITHM he can enter the formula he is currently working on.

We said that the user can vary the width of the columns to accommodate his requirements. A column can be one or more characters wide as defined by him through his cursor. Ten character columns are often found in applications.

The spreadsheet software allows for scrolling columns and rows through the screen or calling them in a menu-like manner as pages.

At the beginning of a session, the spreadsheet starts by presenting the user with a blank worksheet organized into rows (tuples) and columns (attributes). The user sets up his worksheet on the screen just as he would on ledger paper.

We already spoke of the first Multiplan frame presented in Figure 11.1. In this we see seven columns numbered across the top and 20 rows numbered on the left. This is only part of the entire worksheet which is 63 columns wide and 255 rows long. Such a video screen is the window onto the worksheet; the user can move it around to see the rest of the full spreadsheet page.

At the bottom of this screen is a list of commands the user can choose from to build his worksheet and manipulate it:

COMMAND: **Alpha Blank Copy Delete Edit Format Goto Help Insert Lock Move Name Options Print Quit Sort Transfer Value Window Xternal**

Under the commands is a message from the computer that tells the user what to do next: select a command.

For example, let's assume the user selects the ALPHA command which allows him to enter alphabetical or numerical text. To do so, he types on the top row the names of the cost chapters he is considering, say, in a mangement accounting application.

1	2	3	4
FACTORY	**DIRECT LABOR**	**DIRECT MATERIAL**	**OVERHEAD**

He then continues using the ALPHA command and enters the names of the production facilities in the first column. If necessary, he can widen the column to accommodate long words.

1
FACTORY
Alpha
Beta
Gamma
Delta
:
:

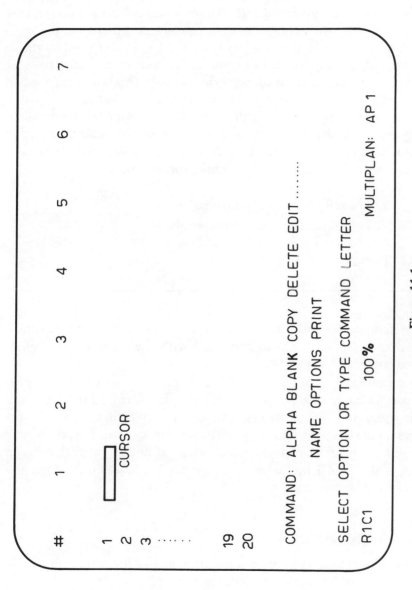

Figure 11.1

Then, in the expense column, he can enter the data for each of the factories. This is done by the VALUE command which allows him to enter numbers or formulas for specific locations on the worksheet.

These locations are called *cells*. There is one cell on the screen that is highlighted by the cursor, and data can be entered only in the highlighted cell. The highlight marker is moved from cell to cell by direction keys on the keyboard. For some cells, the user may wish to enter reference formulas instead of numerical values. This is necessary when the numbers in these cells depend on numbers in other cells.

The user can move the highlight marker to enter the formula. In doing so, he must highlight each element of the formula, connecting them with mathematical symbols from the keyboard. Say, for example, that we wish to link cells creating a formula that:

equals the contents of a cell three rows above

plus the contents of a cell seven rows above.

In Multiplan programming this is written:

$$R [-3] C + R [-7] C$$

The reference formula in Figure 11.2 shows the relative positions of the cells. This is easy to construct with the highlight marker. It can be copied with the COPY command.

The examples of Multiplan implementation we just reviewed help to program engineering or scientific formulas, financial models, forecasting and planning projects, and other applications. Spreadsheet programming permits tailoring software for specific purposes. The end-user does not need to know classical computer programming in order to do it. All he needs to know are his requirements and the problems he wants to solve.

Using Spreadsheet Facilities

Integrated software and spreadsheets put an amazing amount of computer power at the user's disposal. He can:

set up a variety of different models,

simulate decisions, and

see the effects right away.

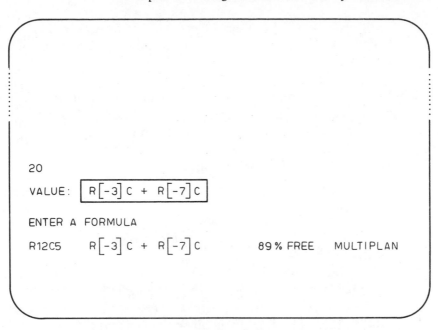

Figure 11.2

This is the sense of the "what if" type of calculation and scenario building. The spreadsheet gives immediate answers to tough questions.

Spreadsheets are syntax-oriented. Each time the user presses a key, they display on the prompt line what can be typed in. The operations are either editing commands that manipulate the contents of the screen, or built-in functions and operators that may be used in arithmetic expressions. Commands include operations for clearing a row, a column, or a specific variable. Commands are also available for replicating the contents of variables, moving information between the screen and file, and for printing. Such commands are entered in the edit line.

Spreadsheets have built-in mathematical and logical functions that enable them to perform fairly complex calculations and analyses. They can also look up values in tables and can be linked to other spreadsheets, thus enlarging the applications domain.

A spreadsheet recalculates by starting at the upper left corner of the sheet. Then, it works its way down and to the right until it reaches the lower right corner of the sheet.

Such systems allow the user to select either of two possible orders—down the columns or across the rows—as the first operation. The functionality supported by spreadsheets overlaps to some extent with that of file, query and menu management systems—and with other types of fourth generation languages.

Every approach has its advantages. Spreadsheets are very user-friendly and easy to manipulate. Learning them is simple, involving cursor movements, calculating functions, editing, and labels and values. Dedicated keys on the right-hand numeric pad of the keyboard move the cursor in the designated direction. The cursor itself is used in value entry and/or commands to point to the appropriate position.

An entry (or command) is executed when the return key is depressed. With Multiplan, a field is defined by row and column, but the software also allows naming the field. For instance, not only can we multiply fields—R2C11* R 2C12—but also assign a name, such as Total for the totals row.

Multiplan also allows connecting up to eight tables defined within different spreadsheets running on the system. This is very important for management reporting where we are interested in summary tables, as it permits building up an hierarchy of eight different layers of spreadsheets.

Table 11.1 Features and facilities supported by Multiplan.

1. General Issues
   1.1 Computation
   1.2 Text handling
   1.3 Use of English words for commands
   1.4 Use of English formulas
   1.5 Alphabetical/numerical sorting
   1.6 Ability to build formulas by highlighting cells
   1.7 Command prompting

2. Formatting and Display Options
   2.1 Windows (up to eight)
   2.2 Full-screen display of formulas in worksheet
   2.3 Variable column width:
      all columns
      individual columns
   2.4 Alignment options (up to three)
   2.5 Format options (up to nine)
   2.6 The user can fix decimal point
   2.7 Commands permitted in numbers

3. Printed Report Options
   3.1 Variable margins
   3.2 Automatic pagination (breaking worksheet into pages)
   3.3 Print formulas

Table 11.2 Functional operations available with Multiplan.	
Facility	No. of Options
1. Cell referencing methods: naming, relative reference, absolute reference	3
2. Arithmetic functions (SUM, AVERAGE, SQ. RT)	16
3. Trigonometric functions (SINE, COSINE, etc.)	4
4. Conditional functions (IF-THEN, AND, OR, etc.)	8
5. Table functions (LOOKUP, INDEX)	2
6. Financial functions (NET PRESENT VALUE)	1
7. Statistical functions (STANDARD DEVIATION)	1
8. Error functions (NA, ERROR)	1
9. String functions (string length, mid-string, etc.)	5
10. Other functions (row, column)	2

If the end-user is relatively inexperienced, prompting can be a great help. Through prompting, the computer gives the user a choice of answers or commands. Table 11.1 identifies the most important features offered by a spreadsheet, in this case, Multiplan.

The range of supported services is important in case the user has a fairly complex forecasting and modeling function to perform wherein strictly mathematical capabilities will not suffice.

For the more expert end-user, further functional operations are available as shown in Table 11.2. Further breakthroughs in expanding programming limits were presented by Lisa and integrated software offerings: Vision, TK! Solver, Lotus 1-2-3, Knowledge Man, MBA.

There are rules to be observed in working with spreadsheets to obtain good results. For instance, it is advisable to keep Multiplan presentations no larger than DIN A4. This means using paging—as with Videotex—with no rotating screens. Design-wise, a good way to look at this issue is to think of the 80-column printer.

When rules are observed, the facilities become more agile and more productive. Rules are also necessary because of the polyvalence of the new tools. Integrated products for management come in the form of calc, graph, and word processing.

The user can show financial figures on screen and print, together with accompanying text and graphic presentations. He can experiment with returns on investments, life cycle calculations, and discounted cash flows. He can sort multiple equations, using "if" conditions, and chart the results. He can even make technical calculations such as building logical circuits by combining spreadsheets (Figure 11.3).

WE CAN BUILD UP LOGICAL CIRCUITRIES

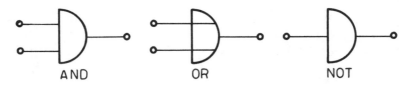

AND   OR   NOT

BY COMBINING SPREADSHEETS

ALSO CIRCUITRY CALCULATIONS

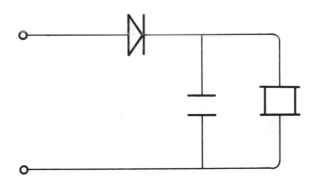

DIODE IS A NON-LINEAR ELEMENT:

    IF CURRENT NON-ZERO.......

    THEN . . . . . .

Figure 11.3

Alternative Possibilities with Spreadsheets

Practically all spreadsheet offerings make feasible cash flow analysis and forecasting; pricing studies; experimentation with profitability; purchase/leaseback analysis; income statements and balance sheet projections; budget planning and consolidation; studies on acquisitions and mergers; or more technical data such as material and labor requirements planning, manpower assignments, resource allocation, the depreciation of equipment, engineering calculations, and so on. There are, however, major differences in terms of the tools supported by each offering.

For instance, many spreadsheets do not allow placing commas (dividing points) in numbers, while others permit producing reports that are properly formatted, with commas and decimal points correctly aligned.

When preparing large worksheets, the user will find it useful to break the sheet up into separate pages. Just the same, he will appreciate a text calculation capability which permits him to set up formulas that print out relevant text.

Such presentation tools are enriched with the second generation of spreadsheets and help differentiate Multiplan from VisiCalc. Supported facilities are further extended with integrated software which incorporates a significant amount of databasing capabilities.

TK! Solver was designed by Bricklin, an MIT graduate and inventor of VisiCalc, primarily for engineering applications. It can run on most PCs with the Intel 8086 family of microprocessors.

TK! Solver and all other Integrated Software offerings have a multitude of arithmetic and trigonometric functions. It also includes an extensive set of functions for operating on numeric and string data.

An application which I did with Software Arts involved seven different key variables to be combined in the study of engineering alternatives in motor design: rotation in cycles per minute, speed, gasoline consumption, effects on steering capability, skidding from applying the breaks on wet surface, and the like.

To show the versatility of integrated software, another application concerned a banking environment and involved:

loan preparation

modeling for experimentation

amortization schedules

loan control

follow-up on client repayment

form printing and reporting

transmit to host computer.

Learning to Use Computer-based Tools

Integrated software handles more extensive worksheets than the typical calc: for instance, 511 rows by 128 columns. In this enlarged spreadsheet, information from one program can be merged with data from another. The system provides virtual memory management to ensure that the entire worksheet can be used with no performance degradation. It also supports cursor movement via a mouse.

A very important feature is that it combines data from different worksheets automatically. Another vital tool is the management of windows.

New products come with rectangular blocks, or windows. Thus, they let users run several different programs at once, each displayed in a separate section of the video screen. Typically, such programs allow users to split their screens into windows. They also attempt to address two fundamental challenges: How to get the same program to run on machines put out by different manufacturers, and how to swap information smoothly between different programs.

Integrated software features simplify entering data, formulas and labels. Calculations are performed by row, column or depth-first techniques.

Easy-to-employ display attributes are provided (including scaling), as well as a thorough set of instructions. There is a descriptive command menu, automatic text formatting, background printing, and support of the mouse to scroll, move, copy, delete, and enhance text.

These programming systems permit attribute assignment on a range basis, and provide powerful delete functions by character, word, line, sentence, paragraph, area, and document.

They use the date for headers and footers; insert actual database tab separations into text; and can present historical information on document preparation. The database uses columns and column headings as fields and rows for records.

Spreadsheets and integrated software support a complete structured programming language. For instance, Knowledge Man, by International Software Enterprises, includes:

1. All of the user arithmetic and logical operators
2. The major control structures with arbitrary levels of nesting:

    if-then-else-endif

    while-do-endwhile

    test-case 1-case 2-...
3. Table fields available as variables
4. Additional global or local working variables
5. One and two dimensional arrays
6. Up to 26 arguments in a procedure.

Any Knowledge Man capability—from creating records and calling up report forms to doing whatever is required in a given procedure—can be invoked from a program.

The user can sort, select and create subjects to design reports. The command file gives the user a lot of power. One of the important display characteristics is the ability to dissociate the scratch pad function from menu selection, and menu selection from reporting. Another characteristic is the simultaneous presentation of tabular data and of the corresponding graphs. This is done with color, smooth scrolling, and a lack of jittering.

Menumaster of Borland International allows the free definition of menus according to the user's personal requirements concerning function and design. Programs can be started and complicated command sequences executed through pushbuttons. Most importantly, the user need not have prior knowledge of the commands at his disposal. The system provides him with some options, of which he chooses the ones he needs.

The classical command sentences have been substituted by a comfortable, menu-driven input. Also:

Screen formats can be freely defined without being bound to a given schema.

Menus call-up other menus parametrically.

All screen attributes are implemented.

Every menu or command can be protected through a codeword against unauthorized usage.

The system looks after a save connection of programs among themselves and controls the data exchange in the files.

Input errors of the user or program rundowns can be caught.

There are prompts and callable help explanations for user guidance.

Statistical analysis is one of the strong points of spreadsheet programs. At a single command, they offer the user full statistics for numeric fields in a table. He can obtain an analysis for a chosen subset of records, and request statistics at multi-level control breaks. Such results are the more impressive as these routines operate on microcomputers.

Both integrated software and the simpler spreadsheet alternatives help the user avoid time-consuming calculations while comparing different alternatives through an "as if"-type experimentation. Evaluation of alternatives can be designed according to the user's own needs— by himself.

In this manner, alternative solutions for budgets, forecasts and cost comparisons can be created and calculated within minutes. The user can move the cursor at any time to any cell on the working sheet, while single or multiple cells can be protected from writing-in through specific commands.

It is also possible to handle special effects such as color and blinking and to configure the system with any of the standard terminal drivers. Typically, spreadsheet programs give the user complete control over printed form layouts. He can define titles and text wherever he likes on a form, print whole forms or fill in preprinted forms, and route reports to disc files as well as to the printer.

Spreadsheets and integrated software are equally flexible with softcopy and hardcopy presentations. Since every effort has been made in their design to simplify the man-machine interfaces, the end-user can employ them just as easily as a professional programmer.

We are entering an era of self-service in computing.

Chapter 12

LINKING THE PC TO THE MAINFRAME

Introduction

Effective personal computing is inseparable from the communications system to which it is attached. The system should provide both real-time and store-and-forward capabilities, with little distinction between the two. It should support not only data communications but also text, voice, and graphics. It should be able to combine the system components in any way desired by the user.

Advanced features are not only welcome but necessary. The system should, for instance, be able to embed voice annotations in text as well as graphic images at particular points in a text or data segment. Also, the range of media supported should be extensible, thus providing for modularity and flexibility as new technologies come along.

The communications system should support both local and wide area transmission, provide for error control, and assure recovery. Recovery may involve data, text, graphics, stored voice, and moving pictures.

This is a great departure from the past. For over 20 years, data communications planning focused merely on equipment and costs rather than on identifying opportunities. Now not only do we have to plan specific facilities, but we also must develop strategies for exploiting them. We must also calculate the potential impact of our computers and communications resources.

Since we must plan for corporate survival and profits, what value should we assign to performance requirements like response time, capacity, recovery, noise sensitivity, message error rate, reliability, and uptime? What policies and procedures are necessary to integrate computers, databases, and communications facilities to produce a cost/effective network?

One of the key topics in answering the last query is the micro-computer-to-mainframe link. The standalone WS can give assistance up to a point. Its value increases multifold if it can reach online—in a way clear to its user—the IE of the corporate mainframes and of public databases.

Protocols, Modems, Networks

Protocols are formal conventions guiding the transmission and handling of information. They are implemented in the computers or other units connected to the network to help control data transfer from one device to another using the facilities offered by hardware and software elements.

Protocols function at various levels, from lower level byte and packet transport to higher level database access in the applications layer. In both cases they are an integral part of all types of computers and communications networks. The formalisms supported by protocols help regulate, among other areas, flow control and error detection.

Protocol formality and standardization are most important. Protocols must be compatible for each layer of the ISO/OSI model to communicate with its corresponding layer residing in other equipment. This can be achieved by adopting the same protocol at each corresponding level or by performing appropriate protocol transformation at a gateway.

The International Standards Organization (ISO) worked on the specifications of a layered solution to networking. Known as the Open Systems Interconnection (OSI), this is composed of seven layers.

The first and lowest layer is *physical*. The modulation/demodulation (modem, dataset) equipment which constitutes this layer interfaces between the PC (or other terminal) which works in a digital mode and the telephone lines which transmit information in analog form.* To communicate over a telephone line, the computer or terminal at either end must be equipped with a modem. The modem converts binary data coming from the terminal (or computer) to analog signals suitable for transmission over a voice line (and vice versa).

Let's repeat this reference. While protocols are *logical* entities, modems are *physical* devices. They constitute the first layer of the ISO/OSI architecture.

The goal of a modem is to permit terminal-to-computer and computer-to-computer communication over a telephone line. The

---

*See also "Handbook of Data Communications," 1985, same author, same publisher.

primary function is the modulation/demodulation of carrier signals so that digital information may be transmitted over an analog communications link, usually a conventional voice grade line.

The reason for using modems is economic. They allow information to be moved, on demand, from one place to another at a very low energy cost. They modulate telephone transmission frequencies at the sending side of the message and demodulate them at the receiving side. There are different types and speeds of modems available which operate differently than the asynchronous modems described in the preceding paragraphs. However, asynchronous (nonsynchronous, start/stop) modems are the most frequently used.

The other six layers in the ISO/OSI model are *logical.* The second layer is the *data link.* Different protocols can serve it: start/stop, binary synchronous, SDLC/HDLC. (SDLC—standard data link control—has been promoted by IBM, and HDLC—highler level data link control—by ISO. They both work with packet switching.)

Only 10 years ago, logical solutions to data communications problems were largely limited to the choice of a data link. Today, there is no more reason to worry about link protocols. We have the technology to handle any data link in a layered manner with replacements based on the same hardware.

The third layer of ISO/OSI is *networking.* The international standard protocol is X.25. This layer is composed of two sublayers: routing, and either virtual circuit or datagram. Routing is very important, particularly in a mesh network, as it assures alternate paths in case of out-of-order situations or congestion.

Virtual circuit (VC) and datagram are alternatives. They both address themselves to the packet switching discipline but differ in terms of the facilities they support. One difference is packet size. Other things being equal, VC—usually a bit stream protocol—handles larger packets than the byte-oriented datagram. More important is the fact that with VC the responsible entity for out-of-order situations and lost packets is the network. With datagrams, the responsibility is with the data terminating equipment (DTE).

The fourth layer in ISO/OSI is *transport* which looks after flow control, congestion, and the DTE connection. (The latter case is a communications window.)

The top three layers of ISO/OSI are also logical but are situated in the data terminating equipment. The fifth is *session* control. It establishes and maintains the communications session.

The sixth is *presentation* control which assures the finer programmatic interfaces for session establishment and maintenance. Great interest in the standardization effort has centered on this layer. Most notable is the North American Presentation Level Protocol Syntax (NA/PLPS) which standardizes videotex communications.

The seventh and last layer of ISO-OSI is oriented to *the user* and his *applications*. This means many things, many conceived and appreciated differently by different people.

We have thus seen that there are six logical layers, each supported by the appropriate protocol. Some layers are higher than others. By consequence, we have higher and lower level protocols. The term "low level protocol" identifies formalisms close to the line discipline, and is used to transport groups of bits (or bytes) through the network.

A low level protocol is not aware of the meaning of the bits being transported. A high level applications protocol knows more about them as it uses the bits to communicate about remote actions.

At the lowest level (physical), high performance is achieved through hardware technology. The next higher level (data link) has accumulated enough experience to permit the simplification of its protocol(s). The protocols for the next layers are designed to take advantage of and preserve the special capabilities of the level to which they belong.

This reference exemplifies how valuable *layering* is as a design issue. It is a technique to assure the logical independence of network modules so that different communications subnetworks, interprocess communications, and data management functions can be altered with minimum disruption.

Planning for Data Communications

Communications technology creates a nation that is a closer, interdependent entity. At the same time, the personal and business lives of the communications facilities' users become more complex. Because of this, high quality communications services become pressing.

International firms aim to have their services linked by a sophisticated global communications network, to hold together their operations, and to respond to their clients' changing needs. National firms do the same for their coast-to-coast operations. The consumer's goal is communications oriented: toward public databases, company offices, financial institutions, merchandizing firms, and other consumers.

Thus, we must develop policies and procedures to assure:

1. Uniform means of dealing with *total* corporate communications requirements.
2. Multifunctionality in implementation.
3. Financial savings from shared communications facilities.
4. Enhanced communication between business units—even seemingly unrelated ones.
5. Support for future applications.

First, the fundamentals. At the base of all transmission and switching is *space, frequency,* and *time division* multiplexing. However, transmission technologies are evolving. So, it is a good policy to carefully analyze what technology offers in terms of cost/effective solutions *now,* and how these solutions will look in the near future. Both current and future possibilities should be examined. Ten years ago it would have been senseless to suggest high capacity pumping through satellites, today, for long haul datacomm networks, it has become a viable alternative.

Coaxial cable has become a popular broadband medium in LAN because of its capacity, low error rates, and configuration flexibility. Something similar can be said of twisted wire for baseband solutions. (Broadband and baseband are signalling techniques which are independent of the physical medium.)

A communications network can be *local* (office level, a building, a group of buildings; *metropolitan* (say, Manhattan, or the Boston area); *long haul* (from intercity to nationwide and global). The applications domain for these networks includes electronic mail, distributed data processing, distributed databases, word processing, file transfer, and remote data entry.

Taking advantage of such facilities means creating improvements in managerial and clerical productivity. With information systems resources connected through a network, a valid architecture should support:

1. Distributed databases
2. Distributed communications
3. Distributed processing
4. Peer-to-peer handling

5. Network control center
6. Security (sign on, password(s))
7. Program confinement
8. Controlled data access (authentication, authorization)
9. Encryption
10. Gateways to other networks (X.25, SNA, et al.).

These are the basic ingredients of networking, creating a web of machines linked through a flexible communications medium toward a goal. Such a network cuts across geographical, hierarchical, and functional lines, offering each individual the ability to increase his personal productivity.

However, the effectiveness of a network is limited by constraints imposed by the medium itself and by the users. The challenge is to extend current communications capabilities in terms of speed, accuracy, flexibility, and numbers of personnel and machines. We must design in a way to increase the organization's ability to take advantage of computers and communications technology. Value added networks aim to answer this goal in a communications environment. Personal computing does the same at the WS level.

Personal computers can be linked via telephone lines to databases containing financial and investment data: the Wall Street Journal; Dow Jones News/Retrieval Service; United Press International; Barron's; Data Resources; CompuServe; The Source, and scores of others. Such connections makes easy retrieval of a wide variety of data.

Utility databases display menus for the information they offer. Just one information provider, Dow Jones, has more than 20 databases, including:

Disclosure, a library of financial extracts from reports filed by public companies with the securities and Exchange Commission;

Corporate Earnings Estimator;

Media General; and

Forbes, a listing of comparative data on the top 1,000 corporations as defined by Forbes Magazine.

The user can easily manipulate the wealth of information on his WS. With spreadsheets, capital gains, dividends, turnovers, earnings and other data are easily compared against the investment costs for multiple portfolios. PCs make these tasks easy, fast, and directly controllable.

Value added networks assure a cost/effective substitute to the dedicated lines most organizations employed in the past. They provide not only the transmission facility (backbone network) but also its management. Such include GTE Telenet, Tymnet, IBM's Information Network, RCA's Cylix, and AT&T Information System's Net 1000.

Public value added networks are favored by organizations with numerous locations. National merchandizers, manufacturers and commercial banks use them because it makes sense to have a third party linking computer installations throughout the country. By entrusting part or all of their networking needs to a third party, companies reduce their involvement in network management and the cost of required personnel. Hardware and software of the value added communications services is located on customer premises and is accessible to the vendor.

Value added networks provide a uniform means of dealing with total corporate communications requirements. They assure financial savings from shared communications facilities and economics of scale; feature multifunctionality; and by balancing the load among different users, they free them of the most common performance constraints.

Value added networks have offered electronic mail facilities since the late 1970s. Today, emphasis is placed on *computer conferencing*. A computer conference is a continuous meeting in which a series of users are connected. Each time a comment is made, it is automatically sent to all other users, allowing a meeting to take place on an extended basis.

Computer conferencing is a significant enhancement over electronic mail, which itself is an improvement over telex and TWX. Electronic mail has been traditionally supported through terminal-to-terminal solutions that suffer the same problems as telephone, telex, or facsimile.

The newer computer-based message systems (computer mailboxes) function as user-to-user asynchronous solutions, instead of as non-intelligent terminal-based synchronous (simultaneous) systems. The computer serves as a central repository for users, each of whom has a mailbox. The mailbox system is a file system that links at least four distinct fields—to, from, subject, and text. The user is prompted through each field, entering the recipient(s), the subject, and the message. Recipients call the mailbox system at their choice, are given a listing of their messages, and the messages themselves. Computer mailbox and conferencing systems are suited for group interaction, which is now a critical management problem in many organizations.

Mailboxes are valuable for a wide range of tasks, from coordinating meetings to receiving comments on a proposal and reports from a group of people in different locations. Computer conferencing allows more general inquiries for information, responses and annotations running over a longer time period.

This is a different way of saying that the many different technologies for computer communications are complementary, not competitive. No single type is suitable for all purposes. We must study the alternatives; evaluate what they offer and what they cost; and select the one best suitable to our needs.

Connecting PCs and Mainframes

A major factor driving the PC market in Fortune 1,000 companies today is the desire to link micros, minis and mainframes. Management interested in microcomputers recognizes the need to integrate the information resources at its disposition.

PCs, supermicros, minis, and mainframes can be linked through a network. A PC can dump upline or download information for its word processing or spreadsheet software. It has intelligence, storage, a screen, and a keyboard or mouse to actuate the communications commands. The PC can hold the information which it receives in its central memory or, better, a hard disc. For response time reasons, storage to floppy should be avoided. However, personal computing embedded in a WS is better exploited when there are full-scale links between the distributed PC and the mainframe(s).

A typical PC-to-mainframe link is shown in Figure 12.1. A front-end processor (FEP) assures the communications interfaces, including line management and character control. The rearend engine runs the corporate database. It is typically managed by a DBMS.

Different reasons point to this arrangement. First is the satisfaction of the growing ranks of corporate WS users clamoring for more data with which to reach their decisions.

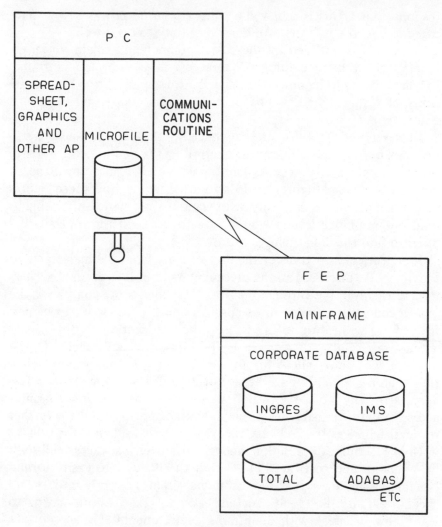

Figure 12.1

Second is the reduction of processing loads on the mainframe. With intelligent WS, the processing job is brought where it belongs—to the workbench.

Third is the easing of programming burdens for the DP staff. As users take more tasks to their WS, applications backlogs shrink considerably.

Fourth is the tailoring of the application itself to the individual needs of the user—with an associated benefit in considerably reducing response time. This is achieved because *computer power is now dedicated to one job,* and therefore has the ability to do it well.

The benefits outlined by these four points help explain why users increasingly want to employ WS to access the corporate mainframe. Efficient communications help the PC to spread through corporations, allowing managers, professionals, and clerks to do their own computer analyses.

However, let's not forget that much of the data needed are still in the mainframe. The executive controlling plan/actual performance by division needs to access the mainframe. A budget analyst who needs last year's expense figures to do a forecast would find those figures in the mainframe. A secretary who wants to use word processing to send out reminder letters would have to draw on the central computer to find the delinquent accounts.

It is necessary to transfer the data directly from the mainframe to the micro. As discussed in the preceding section, the *physical* connection is usually done through an RS 232C cable. More complex is the *logical* connection which must consider the type of work to be performed. We will return to this issue in the next section.

Hardware and software price/performance and technological improvements now allow for the opportunity to put things online that couldn't possibly have been cost/effective, or even done, a few years ago. The potential benefits of online information sharing—accessing data, transferring it, manipulating and storing it for further retrieval—changes this industry the way we have known it for years.

Unlike terminal emulation and file transfer packages, full-scale PC-to-mainframe software links permit the PC user to easily formulate queries and download data from mainframes directly into spreadsheet programs like Multiplan and Lotus 1-2-3 without having to learn how to deal with mainframe environments. These solutions appear promising.

Over the past few years, there has been a gradual integration taking place between data processing equipment and office automation sytstems. Both sides are contributing to the concept of an integrated office.

The combination of the PC/intelligent WS and the host effects a need for more processing power in millions of instructions per second (MIPS) and memory capacity. Existing networks which handle thousands of terminals now have to cope with the addition of PCs. The WS themselves are evolving very fast in terms of databasing and datacomm needs.

Depending on the user organization and its needs, the following five issues can be looked at either as alternatives or as complementary in providing an interconnect facility.

1. Single PC-based WS with communications protocols and hard disc.
2. Clustering software, creating a professional engine out of a supermicro, with two, four, or eight intelligent workstations.
3. Baseband LAN supporting 10 to 30 workstations with the appropriate servers (file, gateway, printer).
4. Broadband cable able to handle 100 to 300 WS into which may be fed several baseband LAN.
5. PBX connections which can use existing twisted wire loops or broadband cable carriers (coaxial or optical fiber).

Integrated PC-to-mainframe links should solve the text/data exchange problems by automatically converting the mainframe information into the form the WS packages can use. The same is valid about the flow from the WS to the central resources.

Even with the best communications link, the WS should have its own database: the *microfile*. This should hold both text/data and programs. In fact, in a LAN situation, programs saturate the communications link much faster than text or data.

Microdatabase systems will not replace mainframe-based solutions. Should this happen, it would be like going back to single-user systems that provide redundant information, nonsharing of corporate resources, and low information systems performance.

The role of mainframes is changing from being data processors to that of assuring a link between PCs, like a large communications switch, and to the effective management of the corporate text and databases running on them. Thus, the background, the backup, the recovery, the text and data warehouse will be assured by the mainframe.

Providing the Logical Link

The preceding section made the point that the physical connection is usually done through an RS 232C cable. More complex is the logical connection. Four main classes can be distinguished:

1. Using the PC as a dumb terminal.

2. Hard disc (at the host) to floppy transfer.

3. Hard disc to central memory (of the WS).

4. Communicating processes at the applications level.

Every one of the connections must be clear to the user.

Without doubt, the simplest approach is to have the WS emulate a nonintelligent computer terminal, which is the way that most computer users interact with commercial databases. In such a timesharing mode, what is required is terminal emulation software on the WS, a modem and a communication line. This is presently the most common form of communication between small and large machines—but not a very effective one. Such a connection only allows the PC to examine the data, not to store them and manipulate them.

One step up is the ability to download data. This permits the end-user to call information from the mainframe and store it. The data is in raw form and software is necessary to get it from storage into the spreadsheet.

Downloading can take place under either No. 2 or No. 3 as mentioned above: hard disc (at the host) to floppy or hard disc to central memory at the PC. The central memory option should be chosen because of response time requirements. Typically, downloading the system will extract portions of, say, sales files from the main computer, restructuring the data into an accessible format for the PC. While this presents no technical problems, management needs to decide not only what data will be allowed to offload, but also what access policies and restrictions should be established.

At the technical side, an improvement over simple downloading is to add software to allow the data to be formatted correctly so they can go from the mainframe to the WS and into the proper slots in the desired program. The inverse procedure should be studied when we wish to use PCs as intelligent data entry machines to upload data to a mainframe database.

Whether downloading or upline dumping, this type of communication requires handshaking protocols at both ends.

A more sophisticated approach is to have the microcomputer and the mainframe run the same programs so that the PC translation of data is not necessary (No. 4 in the list). The WS and the mainframe, for example, may work on the same data, documents or graphics.

Process-to-process communications, like all other modes, can also take place between workstations. Users may, for instance, require joint work on spreadsheets or in text handling. However, text representations and formatting characters vary from package to package. Also, with spreadsheet packages, the data may be represented in different ways. If so, special conversion software is needed to allow such communications to take place.

For obvious reasons, mainframers, PC vendors and software companies are interested in providing interconnect facilities. IBM introduced two desktop machines designed for this: the XT/370 and the 3270 PC, which doubles as a computer and as a 3270 family terminal. The 3270 PC holds four datacomm sessions and two scratch pad sessions. The XT/370 operates under VM.

The XT/370 has standard printed circuit boards (PCB) for communications—but a PCB should be added to the original IBM PC. Other devices can also communicate to an IBM mainframe:

If alien equipment supports the RS 232C, then the connection is only at a physical level.

If a 3274 concentrator is used, it includes data links and teleprocessing capabilities.

If the concentrator is a 3279, the system supports raster graphics.

Also, the 3270 is not a higher level protocol; it is video level-oriented.

In the IBM world the WS linkage can be provided, for example, through a LAN, Ethernet and Wangnet. The same is true for baseband and broadband. It can also be a loop connection (8100, 4700). A peer-to-peer long haul connection can be supported through start/stop, BSC, SDLC, X.25, and X.25 with cryptography.

For a banking environment, IBM bank intelligent terminal communications can be of the 3270 type. Up to four communications can be presented through windows whose dimensions are set by the user. Either of the two scratchpads takes full video.

Indeed, the range of IBM PC offerings is regarded as a key product in the evolution of technology toward a micro-to-frame link. The IBM PC is an important part of the office automation environment because it is the first low-end computer that provides an easy and safe choice for large numbers of sophisticated end-users.

Independent vendors presently offer dozens of products to link a PC to large computers. They are both interactive, with process-to-process orientation, and file-to-file for bulk transfer.

Figure 12.2 demonstrates the structure of a dual protocol. However, the best currently available mechanism for data exchange is the use of file transfer software. At the database level, by providing a uniform filing structure we can simplify the exchange of data. Among current offerings, Management Science America (MSA) in Atlanta, GA, was one of the first to announce a product that tied software running on personal computers to mainframe-resident data.

Online Software International and Softrend market OmniLink, a micro-to-mainframe communications product. ADR/PC, from Applied Data Research, Princeton, NJ, typifies many of the main-

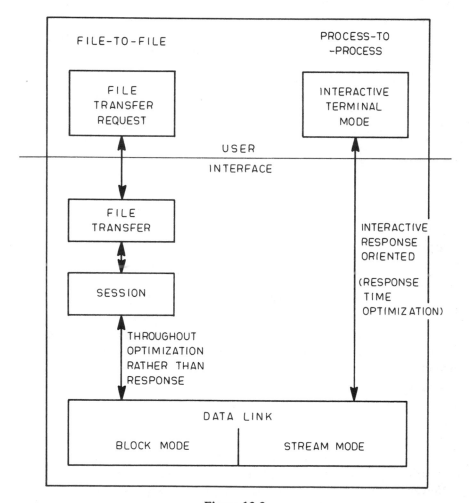

Figure 12.2

frame software link products. While it runs only with ADR mainframe software, such as the ADR/Datacomm/DB relational database management system, it allows the PC user to formulate a simple query, and then downloads the selected data to almost any popular spreadsheet. This provides full security through the data dictionary of the DBMS but does not allow the PC user to update the database.

The package has, however, some unique features: Spreadsheet data can be uploaded to ADR's mainframe-resident Empire decision support system for more sophisticated manipulation. Also, data can be downloaded from multiple mainframes. ADR will soon offer PC components for its program development tools.

Another offering is Interactive PC Link from McCormack & Dodge of Natick, MA. This is one of the most flexible available, capable of directly accessing any IBM mainframe data in VSAM files. Data is downloaded into a Lotus 1-2-3 or other spreadsheet, and the link also interfaces with the company's Millenium financial application software. PC users can use the spreadsheet data to update mainframe files running under Millenium. Data dictionary security is boosted by a PC-mounted hardware component that requires a user ID.

VisiAnswer from Informatics, Woodland Hills, CA, is still another reference. It was developed jointly with VisiCorp, runs with VisiCalc and the rest of the VisiSeries (including VisiOn), and also works with other packages. VisiAnswer can pull data from virtually any IBM mainframe database or application package. The query interface helps unsophisticated users by supplying explanations of each field as the user selects it. It doesn't allow updates. Each diskette is tagged with a user ID number for added security.

PC/204, from Computer Corporation of America, Cambridge, MA, has an easy-to-use interface. To select data, the PC user merely positions a cursor over an empty spreadsheet until the desired column and row headings are filled in. After supplying sample data to ensure the correct selection, the link fills a Lotus 1-2-3 spreadsheet with the downloaded data. Then, it automatically logs users onto the mainframe over asynchronous, error-correcting lines and accepts updates from the mainframe.

Finally, Oracle in Menlo Park, CA, is adding communications to its mainframe relational DBMS. Oracle is today the second most popular relational DBMS for the supermicro, and it works under Unix.

Newer, more ambitious projects focus on programs that down load mainframe files and translate them into a standard Data Interchange Format (DIF) used by most spreadsheet programs. Pathway Designs in Wellesley, MA, offers this capability with its terminal emulation boards.

These are only some examples. We can expect this list to grow considerably with time while the protocols being offered will grow increasingly more sophisticated.

Chapter 13

THE RESPONSIBILITY OF MANAGEMENT

Introduction

The work currently in progress in most industrial and financial enterprises is characterized by a communications-intense environment. This is just as true of distributed information systems as it is of personal computing and office automation.

The completeness of a computers and communications facility is based on three pillars. In order of importance:

1. The expertise of the user organization which proposes to implement it.
2. The will to do the job in a productive, benefit-oriented manner.
3. The software which will be made available.

Such a facility requires clear ideas on how to go about designing, implementing, and maintaining information systems. Solutions must be based not only on short term results but also on expected long term consequences. Solutions which look only after the short term are economically inefficient from the viewpoint of exploitation. They fall short of offering to the organization the results it expects, and fail to fill the voids previous efforts have left.

The choice of hardware is only one of the subjects which should be carefully watched. Software is a much more important issue. Taken together, software and hardware are only part of the process of systems integration.

A determined effort in terms of systems integration should focus both on the total picture and on key technical details such as text/data portability and program compatibility. The more sophisticated the computers and communications aggregate, the more emphasis should be placed on details and—through them—the systems integration.

Finally, an educational effort must include both management—who will be the end-user—and the computer specialists. Lack of appropriate training can easily result in a commensurate loss of control over systems and their performance.

The Management of Change

Modern technology has borne two major trends:

1. An evolution in the use of computer resources, with significant changes in hardware, software, and applications concepts.
2. A reduction by nearly two orders of magnitude of the cost of computer resources.

In the mid-1960s, memory devices cost three to five cents per bit. They now cost less than one-thousandth of a cent per bit.

Putting to work the products technology presents, and doing so in the most efficient manner, calls for *foresight* and *new concepts* to exploit the tools which are being offered. The most vital of these concepts is the steady *process of change*.

The marks of good management are *alertness* to the process of change, *evaluation* on its direction and impact, and *response* through long term measures.

The shift from the short term to the long term brings about the need for new departures. This applies throughout society. Universities, for example, now enter into joint ventures with the biotechnology, computer, and communications industries.

Unless management fully redefines what business a company is in, the company may be out of business. In the financial industry, for instance, in the next few years, we will witness many bank mergers, but also bank failures.

To survive, management must anticipate the impact of change. That means it must:

1. Conceptualize what business is beneficial for the organization. Chances are that this will rest on three pillars:

    market perspective

    human capital

    modern equipment.

2. Re-establish in a documented manner what business the organization is *really* in.
3. Evaluate the difference between projected and current goals.
4. Prepare a plan which permits renewal of the organization in a steady manner without upsetting it.

Skill in long-range forecasting will answer the question: "What's the role of our company in the next 10 to 20 years?" Part and parcel of the answer is a proper *foundation in systems technology*. This is a critical ingredient to the planning process, and it rests on five elements:

personal computing capabilities

online operations: interactive and transactional

systems integration: hardware and software

large computer-driven databases interconnected through datacomm

relationship management with the customer base.

The ability to make factual evaluations and cost/effective implementations, in all five areas, will help develop a transition plan.

A Strategy for Information Technology

The marks of good management are *alertness* to change, *evaluation* of its direction and impact, and *response* through long term measures. The shift from the short term to the long term brings with it the need for new concepts.

The establishment of an effective policy to guide management in the labyrinth of modern information technology calls for precise answers to three questions:

1. What is our strategy for each major business line over the next decade?
   - market goals and objectives
   - product development perspectives
   - cost/effectiveness vs. competition
   - financial goals and objectives
   - major product/service requirements

2. What is the important information technology needs resulting from this strategy?
   - improved productivity
   - competitive service levels
   - product/service capabilities
   - interactive management reporting
   - new information technology-based business

3. What are the relative priorities of the information technology opportunities?
   - competitive positioning
   - integration within the successive layers of strategic objectives
   - identification of high value-added business opportunities
   - flexibility to face technological evolution
   - integration within overall strategy

Information systems must be made in a shrewd, tough, and smart manner. The focus should be on programs and practical decision-making. Matching the efforts of successful competitors in the technological front requires coherent and consistent action. Management must capitalize upon technological opportunities before they become generalized.

At the same time, large investments can prevent further progress. The U.S. Marines Corps, for instance, is said to have 50 million lines of code in applications software written in a variety of programming languages. *Popular Computing* estimated that to rewrite these programs through a slow, redundant, and anachronistic language such as Cobol would call for an expenditure of $30,000,000,000 dollars.

Investments should assure flexibility and the ability to adopt new and more efficient technologies as they develop. Management's role in resolving these strategic issues is ten-fold:

1. Establish information technology directions and policies which result in the resolution of strategic technology issues.
2. Ensure human resources are available to implement these policies and directives.

3. Recognize that information technology has become a growing portion of the organization's value-added stream of market offerings.

4. Provide the capability for product/service differentiation, and assure the responsive introduction of these products and services.

5. Look at technology as a vital tool in increasing the organization's managerial/professional and clerical productivity.

6. Sustain the technical effort required to execute policies and directives in advanced technology.

7. Obtain organization-wide commitment to the policies and directives established by top management.

8. Provide leadership, guidance, responsibility, accountability, and authority.

9. Monitor results of the activities relating to the implementation of these directives.

10. Ensure that critical issues are thoughtfully analyzed and corrective action is taken as necessary.

Particular attention should be paid to the development of a winning strategy for information technology. This requires that the organization justify increasing technological investment and greater systems complexity on the basis of contributions to the value-added structure of the business.

If this approach is not applied, the net result is more technological cost with little return. Figure 13.1 is based on a research correlating technological advances to return on investment.

There are critical questions to be faced in making choices and the implementation of advanced technology. Five basic requirements should be observed:

1. The operating characteristics of the system under development.

2. Technical answers to these characteristics.

3. Underlying support and investments.

4. The way in which needs answered by investments fit with current and projected operations.

5. New approaches/applications/technologies needed to meet these needs.

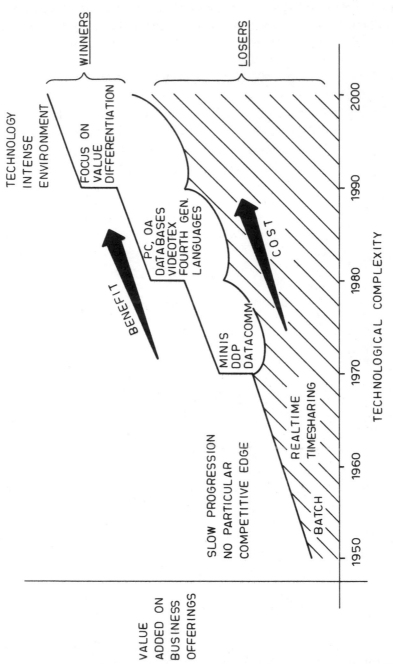

Figure 13.1

Related to these questions are issues of an appropriate development and implementation strategy: new versus enhancement; in-house versus shared; custom versus package. Other challenges include:

What staff resources and skills are necessary for the end-user and the technologist?

Which are the critical support technologies to master (telecommunications networks, PC, software, databases, end-user facilities)?

What is the control action (management authorization, design reviews, budgets, timetables, quality assurance)?

A specific information technology mission should be to analyze issues which are medium to long term (two to five years) and are of strategic importance to the organization.

Top management should focus its attention on interdisciplinary references requiring corporate rather than departmental attention for their successful resolution. The same is valid about the review of shorter term plans and results, particularly those with major strategic implications.

Critical roles in resolving strategic issues are:

Establishing information technology policies and directives which result in the resolution of strategy/technology problems.

Ensuring that human and technical resources are available to implement these policies and directives.

Obtaining corporate-wide commitment to the policies and directives.

Monitoring results of the activities relating to the implementation of policies and directives.

Monitoring activities should be both technical—through design reviews—and financial. The latter should take the form of return on investment studies, always keeping in mind objectives and the maturity period necessary to get results.

In spite of the increasing number of computers within many companies today, the full value of hardware and software—more precisely, the potential return on investment—is often not realized. One of the major reasons for this is that the diverse computing resources cannot share information. System integration studies, data communications protocols, and distributed database disciplines are means for correcting this failure. Recent advances in the area of distributed databases are making it possible for all corporate data to be accessible through any WS.

Return on Investment

The task of assuring a tangible return on investments is quite challenging as this has to be established within the perspectives of a knowledge-oriented society. The investment of Today will bear fruits in the near future, at which time there will be a substantial evolution in structures and values due to technology. Therefore, these issues directly concern the highest levels in the organization—whether they regard only the overall direction to be followed or the overall administration and monitoring of organizational/information systems studies.

Transforming an organization to operate efficiently in a knowledge-oriented society is an imaginative and involved task. Management must shed outdated values, adopt new approaches, and establish new incentives. Among the major contrasts between the old and new environments is the fact that *people, not machines*, are central to productivity. Greater power comes to the managers who possess information and *can turn it into knowledge* for their personnel.

It is increasingly necessary for the information systems strategy to be closely integrated with the overall strategy of the firm. The plans and policies projected for the information system should be developed, implemented, and controlled with great attention.

Within this perspective must be elaborated return on investment (ROI) criteria to help structure an Information Systems Strategy. Three issues are foremost:

First Objective: Do not increase personnel, even if the business increases.

The information system should be tuned to make up for this growth in business activity without requiring an increase in personnel. At the same time, it is necessary that the organization take the needed steps to provide personnel with new functions. A personnel overflow will be created through manpower savings due to computers and communications. (This is the Japanese approach.)

Second Objective: Do not increase the number of computer professionals system analysts and programmers. Instead, use presently available resources more efficiently. In other words, increase quality, not numbers.

This calls for a change in mentality as well as in the tools being used. For instance, if a certain project is programmed in Cobol, it may require 10 people and two calendar years. If programmed in a database language such as Ingres, it might be done by two persons in three months.

Third Objective: Make immediately available information needed by management to improve the mental productivity of the organization.

This goal can be served through electronic mail and videotex—including color and graphics for exception reporting. The same is true of algorithmic approaches evident to management, such as deposits vs. loans and investment. Online access to all decision-oriented information is very important. The analysis of this information should be followed by a comprehensive, user-friendly presentation.

To raise mental productivity, we must find ways to develop new images, promote creative thinking, and facilitate the rapid exchange of information.

Computer-Aided Workplace

The observance of these criteria leads to a *computer-aided workplace* typically served through intelligent WS. Such WS can be based on dedicated personal computers and typically run microfiles, spreadsheets, graphics, electronic mail, word processing, access to databases, and communications.

While computers can play a large role in eliminating routine tasks, clerical productivity is only part of a greater effort to leverage the human mind. The tools which we put at the disposition of managers and clerks should be designed and tuned to serve an intelligent environment. For this reason, they should all be microprocessor-based and therefore intelligent.

A sound policy calls for:

1. One or more dedicated microprocessors per manager and/or clerk.

Equipment costs are relatively low; personnel costs are quite high. It would be silly to divide a microprocessor among users to save a few dollars and lose thousands.

2. High reliability standards and uptime.

This is valid both for software and for hardware, and can properly be served through intelligent WS.

3. Expansion capabilities provided for new applications.
4. An open vendor policy to be assured through commodity choices in microprocessors, OS, languages, database and spreadsheet capabilities.

The choice of specialized WS with nontransportable applications programs and/or basic software is the worst that can be done under current technology. It is a lost investment. This is another reason why PC-based intelligent WS should be used, even if there is a professional engine in the background, thus making feasible the use of dumb terminals.

5. A homogeneous environment is a prerequisite to effective solutions aimed at the enhancement of mental productivity.

Such an environment should be polyvalent and capable of gradually replacing the old systems and procedures.

It is important to provide clear, confident training, to educate and inspire the staff, and to avoid low-key, unprepared ramble that causes confusion and apprehension. The new system must not only work well, but it must also be comprehensive and coherent.

Information is extracted from data. Knowledge is retained information adapted to the job to be done. *ROI evaluations should be based on the acquisition and use of knowledge.*

Another important issue to be considered in this connection is the *maturity period* in reaping benefits from the implementation of technology. There is a three-year period necessary for the maturity of an office automation system as shown in Figure 13.2. It is fully confirmed by research involving the following insurance firms:

Aetna Insurance
American States/Lincoln Insurance
Commercial Union
Continental Insurance
Firemen's Fund (American Express)
SAFECO
Saint Paul Insurance
Travelers Insurance.

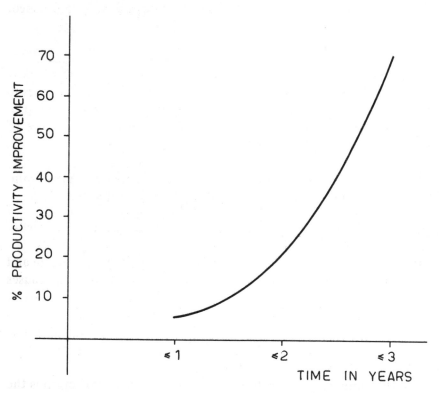

Figure 13.2 Office automation. Results in insurance companies.

While the study involved the insurance sector, this is a business environment by excellence. The result is therefore applicable to other industries, if just generally.

A distributed environment is a prerequisite to office automation so that the same workstations can be used for a broad range of implementations. This multifunctionality is effectively assured through 4GL and associated software—but it also requires system integration capabilities.

INDEX